Cambridge Elements

Elements in Gender and Politics
edited by
Tiffany D. Barnes
University of Texas at Austin
Diana Z. O'Brien
Washington University in St. Louis

GENDERED JOBS AND LOCAL LEADERS

Women, Work, and the Pipeline to Local Political Office

Rachel Bernhard
Nuffield College, University of Oxford

Mirya R. Holman
Hobby School for Public Affairs, University of Houston

Shaftesbury Road, Cambridge CB2 8EA, United Kingdom

One Liberty Plaza, 20th Floor, New York, NY 10006, USA

477 Williamstown Road, Port Melbourne, VIC 3207, Australia

314–321, 3rd Floor, Plot 3, Splendor Forum, Jasola District Centre, New Delhi – 110025, India

103 Penang Road, #05–06/07, Visioncrest Commercial, Singapore 238467

Cambridge University Press is part of Cambridge University Press & Assessment, a department of the University of Cambridge.

We share the University's mission to contribute to society through the pursuit of education, learning and research at the highest international levels of excellence.

www.cambridge.org
Information on this title: www.cambridge.org/9781009482899

DOI: 10.1017/9781009482875

© Rachel Bernhard and Mirya R. Holman 2025

This publication is in copyright. Subject to statutory exception and to the provisions of relevant collective licensing agreements, with the exception of the Creative Commons version the link for which is provided below, no reproduction of any part may take place without the written permission of Cambridge University Press & Assessment.

An online version of this work is published at doi.org/10.1017/9781009482875 under a Creative Commons Open Access license CC-BY-NC-ND 4.0 which permits re-use, distribution and reproduction in any medium for non-commercial purposes providing appropriate credit to the original work is given. You may not distribute derivative works without permission. To view a copy of this license, visit https://creativecommons.org/licenses/by-nc-nd/4.0

When citing this work, please include a reference to the DOI 10.1017/9781009482875

First published 2025

A catalogue record for this publication is available from the British Library

ISBN 978-1-009-48289-9 Hardback
ISBN 978-1-009-48285-1 Paperback
ISSN 2753-8117 (online)
ISSN 2753-8109 (print)

Cambridge University Press & Assessment has no responsibility for the persistence or accuracy of URLs for external or third-party internet websites referred to in this publication and does not guarantee that any content on such websites is, or will remain, accurate or appropriate.

Gendered Jobs and Local Leaders

Women, Work, and the Pipeline to Local Political Office

Elements in Gender and Politics

DOI: 10.1017/9781009482875
First published online: February 2025

Rachel Bernhard
Nuffield College, University of Oxford

Mirya R. Holman
Hobby School for Public Affairs, University of Houston

Author for correspondence: Rachel Bernhard,
rachel.bernhard@nuffield.ox.ac.uk

Abstract: Men from business are overrepresented in local politics in the United States. The authors propose a theory of gendered occupations and ambition: the jobs people hold – and the gender composition of those jobs – shape political ambition and candidate success. They test their theory using data on gender and jobs, candidacy and electoral outcomes from thousands of elections in California, and experimental data on voter attitudes. They find that occupational gendered segregation is a powerful source of women's underrepresentation in politics. Women from feminine careers run for office far less than men. Offices also shape ambition, candidates with feminine occupations run for school board, not mayor or sheriff. In turn, people see the offices that women run for as feminine and less prestigious. This Element provides a rich picture of the pipeline to office and the ways it favours men. This title is also available as Open Access on Cambridge Core.

Keywords: gender, occupation, political ambition, local politics, role congruity, gender stereotypes, gender role theory, femininity, masculinity

© Rachel Bernhard and Mirya R. Holman 2025

ISBNs: 9781009482899 (HB), 9781009482851 (PB), 9781009482875 (OC)
ISSNs: 2753-8117 (online), 2753-8109 (print)

Contents

1 A Theory of Gendered Role Congruity and Local
   Political Leaders   1

2 Measuring Gender and Occupation among Local Leaders 11

3 Gendered Occupational Segregation Shapes
   Who Runs and Wins Local Office   19

4 Gender-Segregated Jobs Influence Perceived
   Occupational Femininity and Win Rates   32

5 It's Not What You Know, It's Who You Know:
   Why Business Leaders and Teachers Dominate Local
   Politics   38

6 Voters See Some Local Offices as Feminine
   and Less Prestigious   48

7 Work Is Gendered, Politics Is Gendered, and Ambition
   Is Gendered   59

   Appendix A   64

   References   66

1 A Theory of Gendered Role Congruity and Local Political Leaders

> Someone said to me, 'women do all the work. They do non-profit work and volunteer and take care of the children and the elderly. And then they turn around and have to be supplicants to the men in power. 'Please, sir, can we have some money for our schools and the disabled?' I hate that. We need to stop being the supplicants and actually be the ones in power. Maybe men should be the ones doing bake sales to get money for their guns and wars. Why should a school even need a bake sale?
>
> – *S., City Councillor*

The ideal political candidate in the United States is well connected, organised, ethical, hardworking, and prepared to handle long hours, intense interaction with people, and difficult situations. Nurses, teachers, and social workers all easily meet these criteria. Why, then, are our ballots filled with lawyers, bankers, and business managers? We propose a *gendered theory of occupation and political representation* and test it in the local political environment of the United States. We show that the alignment of a candidate's gender, the gender typically associated with the candidate's occupation, and the office they are seeking all interact to influence candidate emergence (*who runs*) and voter choice (*who wins*). As a result, ballots for mayor, city council, and sheriff are filled with men with experience in business, law, and science. But in other local offices, such as school board, community services director, and city clerks, we see a robust group of teachers and non-profit leaders running for office. The gender segregation of these occupations thus passes on to produce further gender segregation in who holds local offices.

Running for political office is an extraordinarily rare activity. Less than 2 per cent of Americans will ever become a political candidate. Those who do choose to run are exceptional in many ways: they are wealthy, have access to a wide set of professional and financial resources, and are highly motivated (Bernhard, Eggers, & Klašnja, 2024; Bernhard, Shames, and Teele, 2021; Conroy & Green, 2020; Sweet-Cushman, 2020b). That white men make up most of the people who run for and hold office is one of the most reliable and most damning features of modern American democracy.

In this Element, we provide four new lenses through which we can examine the root causes of the overrepresentation of white men in office. First, we draw on the Census to document the occupational backgrounds of more than 37 million men and women in the general population in California, and combine it with data on nearly 100,000 candidates for and winners of California political offices. The wealth of data provides a much richer and wider view of how ordinary residents run for office. By comparing candidates and winners to the general population, we can see the gendered and occupational pathways to local offices in new and exciting ways. Second, we complement our quantitative data with qualitative studies of prospective candidates' decision-making processes about whether to enter politics, giving us a deeper sense of what those numbers actually mean. Third, we examine a much wider set of offices than researchers traditionally use when they examine gender, occupations, class, local politics, or political engagement more generally. Finally, we combine this broad set of observational data with innovative surveys and experimental work to show that the public understands occupations, offices, and the combination of the two as highly gendered. The combination of these approaches allow us to demonstrate that *opting into politics is rooted masculine occupations*, that *the pool of candidates fails to represent the gender and occupation composition of the population*, and that *the sources of power in local politics largely remain in the hands of men from a narrow set of masculine occupational backgrounds.* The offices that women do run for are seen as *more feminine and less prestigious.*

Women hold less than a quarter of seats in the US Congress, less than a third of state legislative seats, and only one in four mayors of large cities are women (CAWP, 2020; de Benedictis-Kessner, Einstein, & Palmer, 2023); similar levels of underrepresentation are seen among women in municipal government in other countries (Funk, 2015; Tolley, 2011). Women of colour are particularly underrepresented in US political office, making up less than 10 per cent of both the US Congress and state legislatures. And, of course, the United States has never elected a woman president and only one woman has served as a vice president; this has normative consequences (is a democracy democratic if half of the population is routinely excluded from power?[1]) and means that political institutions in the United States are less efficient, solve fewer problems, and are seen as less legitimate and trustworthy. The majority of what we know about

---

[1] As Elsässer and Schäfer (2022, p. 1363) note, 'The numerical underrepresentation of a certain group in legislative bodies is not in itself a normative case for their equal or proportionate representation – though it may point at existing forms of structural discrimination.'

women in politics is among the very elite: women who run for national and high-level state offices. But more than 95 per cent of the elected offices in the United States are found at the local level, and we know much less about this group, particularly offices like school board, county sheriff, and city treasurer.[2]

Women's lack of access to political office implicates underlying social and cultural ideas about gender. Every society is organised around gendered social roles, which are patterns in behaviours and attitudes exhibited by men and women (Eagly & Karau, 2002). Gender role theory argues that society trains men and women to fulfil specific, socially constructed roles (Blackstone, 2003; Eagly & Karau, 2002; Gould, 1977; Schneider & Bos, 2019). A consequence of these gender roles is that women are socialised and expected to be 'good at' tasks associated with the private sphere: for instance, taking care of children, helping others, and collaborating to solve domestic problems. Likewise, men are socialised to be 'good at' tasks associated with the public sphere: working outside the home, protecting women and children from outside threats, and providing leadership (Schneider & Bos, 2019).

Socialisation in both childhood and adulthood teaches men and women about appropriate behaviour and goals for their gender (Bos et al., 2021; Diekman & Murnen, 2004). These patterns are reinforced through internal and external social rewards and punishments (G. Bauer & Dawuni, 2015; Cassese, 2019). Researchers talk about those individuals whose appearances and behaviours match their assigned gender roles as being *gender role-congruent*, and those who don't as *gender role-incongruent* (Eagly & Koenig, 2006).

One persistent consequence of social gender roles manifests as occupational segregation by gender. A combination of historical discrimination (Zellner, 1972), the gendered nature of the household and the economy (Gingrich & Häusermann, 2015; Iversen & Rosenbluth, 2008), and gender roles (Diekman et al., 2011) push and pull women into feminine-typed careers like teaching, nursing, and social work, while men are much more likely to become engineers, construction workers, and business owners. Those who conform more highly to their gender roles—for instance, men who are firefighters (working, physically protecting others) and women who are preschool teachers (caring for children, helping others)—fulfil societal expectations and thus tend to be valorised. This means that gender roles push and pull women towards some careers and interests and men towards others (Diekman et al., 2010). Gendered patterns of interest then interact with a gendered economic

---

[2] In the United States, there are approximately 135,000 city elected officials (mayors, city councillors, treasurers, clerks, and more), 127,000 township members, 58,000 county officials, 95,000 school board members, and 84,000 special district members.

system (Rosenbluth, Light, & Schrag, 2004) and historical patterns (He et al., 2019) to structure economic and political patterns in society. One consequence is that women engage in many types of labour in the home for free: 'a third or more of society's work' is performed without compensation by women for their families and communities (Iversen & Rosenbluth, 2013, p. 306).

Gender roles are also racialised. Race, ethnicity, and gender are dominant, intertwined structures in American society (Bejarano & Smooth, 2022; Brown & Gershon, 2016; Carmines & Stimson, 1990; Crenshaw, 1989; Jardina & Piston, 2019; Omi & Winant, 2014). This means that race and gender intersect to place particular burdens on women of colour (Brown & Gershon, 2016; Crenshaw, 1991). Women of colour have long worked outside the home, even as many white women stayed home during the mid-1900s (Goldin, 2021). People understand gender in the context of their own racial and ethnic group, which means that penalties and rewards for gender role violations and compliance are primarily meted out to those within their group (Xiao, 2022). While we do not focus on racial or ethnic segregation in occupations here because occupational segregation occurs primarily by gender, it is critical to remember that what is seen as gender role-incongruent (and therefore punished) will vary by race *and* by gender.

Gender roles shape not just sorting into occupations, but how we think about leadership (Eagly, 2007; Kweon, 2024). Close your eyes and imagine a CEO or leader in a business field. Who do you see in your mind? Does that person have a specific gender? Race? Age? Who we imagine at the 'top' of a field, company, or organisation, be it education, business, or politics, is gendered. Women are not seen as easily occupying masculine or leadership roles (Schneider & Bos, 2019; Schneider, Bos, & DiFilippo, 2022; Sweet-Cushman, 2020a), which include politics (Holman, Merolla, & Zechmeister, 2022; Oliver & Conroy, 2018, 2020). And, the occupations that 'fit' with our views of political leadership are commonly held by men in society, including business leaders and lawyers.

The intertwined nature of social gender roles and views of leadership have consequences for politics, policy preferences, and interest in running for office (Conroy, 2016; Schneider & Bos, 2019; Schneider et al., 2016). Internally, women's socialisation into communal gender roles leads them to seek out positions that involve working collaboratively with others, interpersonal communication, and helping improve society (Diekman et al., 2010; Eagly & Karau, 2002). While these all are activities that *could* be fulfilled by political careers, men and women both perceive political careers to instead fulfil agentic gender roles by seeking power, individual autonomy, and strong leadership (Conroy & Green, 2022; Ohmura & Bailer, 2023; Schneider et al., 2016).[3] Women are thus less likely to see political careers as consistent with their broader socialised career goals (Schneider et al., 2016). However, this field of scholarship has not yet considered whether a candidate's occupation might signal more or less interest in communal activities, or how many local political offices like school board might be seen as more communal (though extensive work has shown that higher-level and executive offices, like the presidency, are seen as more masculine and agentic).

It is not just women's lack of interest that limits their access to politics: the political system itself is also uninterested in women's leadership. External factors, including voter biases, political party behaviour, fundraising, and the campaign environment, also suppress women's political ambition (or inflate men's ambition). For example, Crowder-Meyer (2013) finds that women are less likely to be a part of local political party networks that are used to recruit candidates for office; this is particularly true when local leaders are men. And, because women generally need more encouragement to run for office than do men (Badas & Stauffer, 2023; Karpowitz, Monson, & Preece, 2017; Preece, 2016; Preece, Stoddard, & Fisher, 2016), the exclusion of women from these recruitment networks is doubly damning.[4]

One consequence for politics is that voters then hold beliefs about individual capacity for leadership based exclusively on that individual's gender. These stereotypes can include that women will be better at producing policy in areas like education and welfare, or that men are stronger leaders (Bernhard, 2022; Holman et al., 2018). Because political leadership is associated with the traits and skills that men are socialised to be better at, voters can hold biases against women seeking positions, particularly if those positions are seen as needing strong leadership (N. M. Bauer, 2020a). In previous work, we have shown that these apply across local offices, with voters preferring men for mayoral positions and women for school boards (Anzia & Bernhard, 2022).

Gender stereotypes held by voters serve as a powerful external obstacle to women's political parity. Here, voters use their knowledge about gender in society to infer information about candidates on the ballot, such as that women running for office will be more compassionate and men with be

---

[3] Women in office also behave in ways that are consistent with communal gender roles, including co-sponsoring more, working more frequently across partisan lines, and communicating more with constituents (J. Adams et al., 2023; N. M. Bauer & Cargile, 2023; Holman & Mahoney, 2018).

[4] These issues extend to women's access to campaign finance networks (Barber, Butler, & Preece, 2016; Kettler, 2020) and media coverage (N. M. Bauer, 2022; N. M. Bauer & Santia, 2023; N. M. Bauer & Taylor, 2023).

more assertive and stronger leaders (Barnes & Beaulieu, 2014; N. M. Bauer, 2015; Bernhard, 2022; Holman, 2023).[5] Because stereotypes of men are better aligned with the activities associated with political office, voters thus often believe that men will be better at performing the tasks of that office. Such stereotypes are powerful because they are self-reinforcing and built on behaviours that originate from socialised patterns that begin at an early age (Bos et al., 2021). While scholars have pointed to the fact that voters are more 'tolerant' of the women running for local positions (N. M. Bauer, 2018) and for specific roles like school board (Anzia & Bernhard, 2022) and city clerk (Crowder-Meyer, Gadarian, & Trounstine, 2015), we know much less about how potential candidates and voters weigh gender expectations for the broad set of offices available in local politics.

One way that an individual candidate might demonstrate that she is capable of leadership is by emphasising and listing the previous jobs she has held, such as CEO or business owner, as these provide information to voters about the skills and traits of the candidate. Political consultants are especially aware that this is a problem for women. During a California women's candidate training on 'Assessing the Political Landscape', experienced consultants emphasised the importance of the ballot designation, or listing of occupation on the ballot: 'the public is more skeptical of women's credentials, so it's good to describe your credentials in as interesting and detailed a way as possible' (A., 2/21/16).[6] For local offices, consultants recommended including descriptors such as education (for school board), finance (for comptrollers), and legal experience (for district attorneys). For the ballot designation to be valid, the occupation or activity must have taken place in the last year, so consultants recommended that candidates volunteer or take on part-time work in relevant areas (e.g., running for president of the school's parent-teacher organisation) to ensure the strongest possible (valid) ballot designation.

Both existing scholarship and our own interviews of political consultants thus suggest that gender matters in evaluations of leadership; that men and women are seen as capable of different forms of leadership, and that occupations can provide candidates with an opportunity to overcome these views. We know much less, however, about how gendered occupational segregation shapes who runs for and who wins local office. In this Element, we argue that

---

[5] Explicit voter biases against women, in the form of hostile sexism, can also limit women's success. Much of the work on hostile sexism and voting has focused on national offices (see Cassese & Holman, 2019), but see Cargile and Pringle (2019) for work that suggests a more complicated relationship in the local context, particularly for women of colour.

[6] See Section 2 for a discussion of the origins of these insights.

gender and occupation deeply shape both who emerges as a candidate for office and who is ultimately elected.

A New Theory of Occupational Gender Segregation and Local Politics

Weaving together this literature, we argue that there is a relationship between occupational gender segregation and local politics:

- As a consequence of gendered social roles and gendered occupational socialisation, women systematically emerge as candidates from feminine occupations and for offices seen as more feminine.
- Voters reward candidates whose femininity or masculinity of their occupation matches what they believe to be the work of the specific office.
- Women and candidates with feminine occupations are advantaged only for offices considered less powerful and less important.

Importantly, not all offices are equally associated with specific prototypes and not all occupations are equally advantaged or disadvantaged across specific offices. In Sections 3 and 4, we provide additional evidence for our theory of gendered occupation and political representation by showing that women emerge as candidates primarily from feminine occupations. In Section 6, we use a new survey experiment to show that voters see candidates from occupations dominated by men as better qualified to hold many local offices, including important offices like mayor. In comparison, feminine occupations like educator and social worker are seen as holding and succeeding only as city clerks and on the school board. In this way, masculine occupations open far more doors for political success than do feminine occupations. Our work shows persistent patterns across time, where gender divisions in labour determine perceptions of occupational femininity; occupational femininity shapes the emergence of candidates for local office; and voters use the femininity of occupations as information about the acceptability of candidates for specific local offices.

We test our theory by examining how gender, race, and occupation shape who runs for office and who wins at the local level, using data from all candidates on the local ballot in California from 1995 to 2021 (Anzia & Bernhard, 2022; Bernhard & de Benedictis-Kessner, 2021). In California, each candidate provides their occupation, which is then listed in voter materials and on the ballot, often referred to as a 'ballot designation'. In total, we coded the gender and occupation of more than 99,000 candidates for a wide set of local political offices, from the mayor to city council to sheriff to school board. California provides the ideal environment for examining *who runs for local*

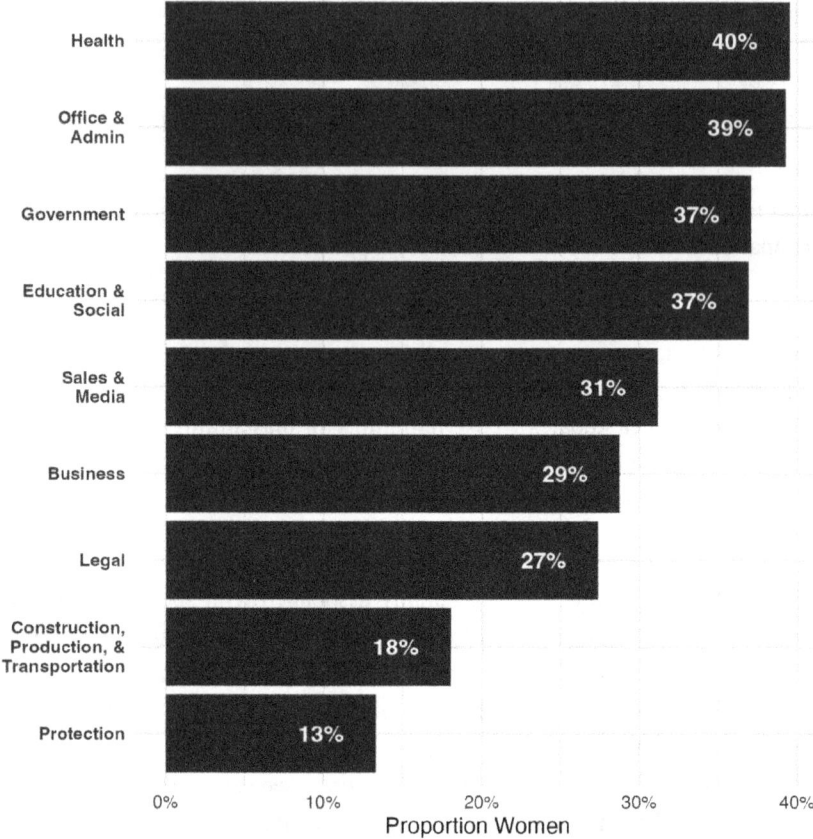

Figure 1 Gender segregation by occupation in the candidate pool mirrors the general population. The percentage of political candidates that are women within each professional sector is shown in white font in each bar. Derived from the California Elections Data Archive (CEDA).

office and who wins, as local elections feature a diverse set of candidates running for local positions that vary in prestige, gender typicality, and electoral environments. We discuss this dataset and our approach of categorising this data in much more detail in Section 2. These occupations vary in their femininity and masculinity; for example, some candidates list occupations like 'preschool teacher and mother' on the ballot, while others might list 'businessman and security guard'.

In Figure 1, we provide a first look at our data on political candidates, broken down by gender and occupation. What we can see already is that gender segregation by professional sector is as noticeable within the candidate pool as it is within the greater population. In the following sections, we explore in greater detail why that might be.

Although local politics offer an ideal opportunity to understand the origins of representation, empirical work examining this topic has been constrained by a host of difficulties: immense variation in electoral institutions and environments across cities, shifting policy challenges within cities over time, and the costs and challenges of collecting data sans standardised record-keeping. Recent work has begun to overcome these challenges (Barari & Simko, 2023; Crowder-Meyer et al., 2015; de Benedictis-Kessner & Warshaw, 2020a), but many major questions remain, including very basic questions about descriptive representation, ambition, and voting behaviour, especially around women in politics. Our work—which combines survey, experimental, and observational data—overcomes some of these limitations and offers a fresh view of one of the most persistent and widespread sources of women's underrepresentation.

Where does the underrepresentation of women begin? One important and yet understudied source is the gender imbalance in who runs for and holds local office. For many candidates, their first run for office will be for a school board or a city council position, even if their career culminates in a national office (Carroll & Sanbonmatsu, 2013; Holman, 2017; Sanbonmatsu, 2006). Women in Congress, from Kay Granger to Dianne Feinstein to Mia Love, started their political careers as city council members or mayors in their hometowns. Other members of Congress have left federal office to seek local office: Los Angeles's first woman mayor, Karen Bass, was first a member of Congress, and Sheila Jackson Lee, a long-time member of the House of Representatives, launched an unsuccessful bid to be the mayor of Houston, Texas. Indeed, local offices are often an end in themselves for many individuals, particularly in smaller towns and cities in the United States (Budd, Myers, & Longoria, 2016; Einstein et al., 2020).

Beyond serving as a pathway to other offices, local politics also is where many of the most pressing issues of our day—like management of restaurant closures and mask mandates during COVID, teaching about topics like LGTBQ + rights and slavery, protections for victims of interpersonal violence, and access to reproductive healthcare—get decided. If women and especially women of colour are excluded from those conversations as elected officials, they remain in the role of 'supplicants' (to the men in power) described by City Councilmember S. above.

Despite the importance of local politics, this topic has historically been understudied by the gender and politics community. While we know that having more women in local politics then leads to more women in state politics and eventually to more women in national politics (Carroll & Sanbonmatsu, 2013), we know much less about what gets women into (or keeps them out of) local politics in the first place. This dearth of knowledge means that we also know very little about the backgrounds and experiences of these women. What one of the co-authors of this Element wrote in 2017 remains true today: 'Indeed, scholars of political science, public administration, and urban studies know very little about even basic information about levels of women's representation, the institutional and demographic factors associated with these levels of representation, or the effects of women's lack of parity on local policy' (Holman, 2017, p. 285). In short, even at the cutting edge of political science work on local politics, we are just starting to know even basic facts like how many women run for a given local office each year, let alone the complex relationships between characteristics like gender, occupation, and political ambition and attainment.

Outline of the Element

We start our discussion in Section 2 with a discussion of the data sources and methodological approaches that we use in the text. In doing so, we outline the challenges associated with studying local politics, including how and where to get data and why our approach is innovative.

In Section 3, we focus on how gender, occupation, class, and resources shape who runs for local office and why. In the section, we first present extensive descriptive information about the share of women as candidates for a wide set of local offices in California and then compare the share of the population, men, and women from different occupations among Californians, candidates for local office, and winners. In doing so, we show a high level of self-selection from the share of an occupation in the general population to candidates and winners, in highly gendered ways. Only a handful of feminine occupations feed into political office, while people (mostly men) run with a wide set of masculine occupations. As a result, feminine occupations are underrepresented among candidates and elected leaders.

How are masculinity and femininity associated with particular occupations and shape candidates for and winners of local office? In Section 4, we draw on a unique survey to first show that the public assigns femininity to occupations by the share of women in those occupations. We then apply those femininity evaluations to occupations in the candidate dataset and show that candidates who list more feminine occupations on the ballot win several types of local elections, even after controlling for time and location-specific factors.

Section 5 takes a deep dive into two occupational categories: business and education. These two groups are overrepresented among local candidates and have specific skills, networks, and stereotypes associated with them that advantage or disadvantage their efforts to seek office. In the section, we look carefully at *how* business leaders and teachers describe themselves on the ballot and how these descriptions convey information about the masculinity and femininity of those on the ballot, contributing to the gender gap in candidates and leaders. We show that men and women from business and education backgrounds are similarly successful in seeking office, but that the two backgrounds provide advantages for specific offices. For example, business leaders win most local offices at higher rates than those with other occupations, while teachers are advantaged for school board – but are *disadvantaged* when seeking offices like mayor or city clerk. Because business leaders are mostly men and teachers are mostly women, men tend to be advantaged when seeking office.

In the last substantive section, Section 6, we examine how voters want leaders who will perform different gender roles for different offices. Using a combination of California election data and a novel survey experiment that asks individuals about their perceptions of different offices and occupations, we show that people's views of a candidate's electability to specific offices are rooted in their occupation (i.e., accountants are seen as particularly electable for treasurer positions and teachers for school board) and that the assessments of these occupations *and* offices are highly gendered such that school boards and clerks are seen as feminine while sheriffs are masculine. We also show that masculinity is highly correlated with prestige, such that the offices that women seek—those seen as feminine—are not considered prestigious.

In Section 7, we conclude by considering what our work says about candidates for office in the United States and around the world. Drawing on comparative work, we consider the ways that our work might translate to other countries—or not—and how factors like sector employment, gender roles, and development play in shaping occupational segregation and women's access to political power. Our work also allows us to consider questions about how voters evaluate other components of a candidate's portfolio or identity, including sexual orientation, disability, age, or immigrant status. What we do and do not know about candidates for local office in the United States can tell us much about representation, equity, and democracy.

2 Measuring Gender and Occupation among Local Leaders

How many women are mayors in the United States? Would you be surprised to learn that no one knows? And no one has the capacity currently to know without calling every city and township and county and school board—all 90,000 local governments in the United States? Both coauthors of this Element have spent substantial time grappling with the lack of data about local government in our professional careers.[7] In this section, we provide information about the data and methods we use in this Element.

One of the downsides of studying inequalities in local politics is that we just do not know a lot about local politics, particularly about how gender operates in these contexts. In many cities and counties, data on elections is not made available to the public, and what is made available often lacks the sort of information that enables easy analysis. For instance, most election data in the United States doesn't contain information on candidate race, ethnicity, or gender. That means that for very basic questions like 'How many women ran for office last year in City X?,' we often can't answer the question without substantial additional work (de Benedictis-Kessner, Lee et al., 2023). Multiply this work by the nearly 90,000 local governments in the United States (Marschall et al., 2011), and one can see that this is a task that requires enormous resources and time.[8]

The challenges associated with collecting, cleaning, and collating local elections or candidate information make recent data innovations by scholars working in this area all the more impressive. One strand of innovations falls under the heading of 'big data'. For many years, scholars working on evaluating the effect of electing women, Black, or Democrat mayors to various offices used a dataset first created by Ferreira and Gyourko (2014), extended by Hopkins and Williamson (2012), extended again by Hopkins and Pettingill (2018), further developed by de Benedictis-Kessner and Warshaw (2016, 2020b), and then used by others (Farris & Holman, 2024; McBrayer & Williams, 2022) to test new questions. Eventually, de Benedictis-Kessner, Lee, Velez, and Warshaw (2023) have filled in the missing pieces to produce a dataset that covers nearly 60,000 local elections over more than three decades in most medium and large American cities. The authors use machine learning algorithms to classify the probable partisanship, gender, and race/ethnicity for candidates for city council, mayor, school board, county commission, and sheriff. Similarly, Kirkland (2021) has built a dataset of mayoral elections over more than fifty years in medium and large cities, including not just race and

---

[7] Throughout the text, we refer to work that we have done previously as 'our' work, even if we have completed that work separately.

[8] Organisations like the Center for American Women in Politics (CAWP, 2019), and some websites, such as Ballotpedia, make some of this data available. But data collection and provision process focuses on larger cities. de Benedictis-Kessner, Lee, et al. (2023) have recently offered a large database of election results for local officials, but it also focuses on larger cities and counties. Organisations like the MIT elections lab offer voter-side information like voter turnout and presidential elections returns at the municipal level, but do not provide the candidate information.

gender but also occupational background and prior political experience.[9] Shah, Juenke, and Fraga (2022) demonstrate that a collaborative project where many researchers participate is an effective ways of generating a large dataset, while Sumner, Farris, and Holman (2020) point to using crowdsourcing to collect large datasets on local politics. These innovations allow scholars today to ask questions about local representation that had previously been confined either to small samples of cities, case studies, or the examination of only the largest cities. Other works, like Farris and Holman (2023b) and Crowder-Meyer (2020), weave together survey and interview data to obtain information on the characteristics and attitudes of difficult-to-study groups like sheriffs and budding political candidates. Even with these advances, however, scholars are still limited in their ability to examine smaller cities or more esoteric forms of local government like city clerk (Crowder-Meyer et al., 2015) or sheriff (Farris & Holman, 2023b; Thompson, 2022).

California stands out as a special case—one widely used by scholars of local US politics—because it has made available a detailed record of local elections from 1995 to 2021[10] through the California Elections Data Archive (**CEDA**). California is also special because its ballots contain *ballot designations*, which contain information on candidates' occupations, which can include jobs held and activities like volunteering and parenting. A wide set of scholarly work uses this data in one form or another (i.e., Anzia & Bernhard, 2022; Atkeson & Hamel, 2020; Einstein, Palmer, & Glick, 2019; Hajnal & Trounstine, 2014; Hankinson & Magazinnik, 2023). This data is not error-free; for example, our previous work has audited and corrected numerous errors in the heavily used CEDA data (Bernhard & de Benedictis-Kessner, 2021).[11] Other states like Louisiana provide detailed information about the gender, race, and party of all candidates for office (Keele et al., 2017), but do not provide occupation information or require that candidates supply such information directly to voters.

CEDA and Census

Our electoral data come from the California Elections Data Archive (CEDA) and cover elections at various levels of government in California from

---

[9] Other scholars focus on a particular set of occupations; for example, a new dataset built by Ba et al. (2023) joins records requests, Census, and voter file data to create demographic and public opinion data on more than 220,000 police officers.

[10] As of July 2023.

[11] Another strand of innovations in local politics addresses issues of producing research in the context of poor and insufficient data. For example, Gunderson et al. (2021) show that after correcting data errors, there is no relationship between transfers of military equipment to local police forces and crime reduction.

1995 to 2021 (Bernhard & de Benedictis-Kessner, 2021). The CEDA dataset includes information on candidates participating in more than 29,000 elections at the county, city, college/school district, and other local levels. These elections range from those for directors of community services districts, who provide services like water treatment and sanitation in medium-size cities, to mayors and city council members overseeing multibillion-dollar budgets in large cities, to school board races in rural areas with only a few thousand residents.

Unfortunately, this comprehensive dataset is not quite as comprehensive as we need to answer social science questions. For instance, it does not contain any data on the gender, race, or ethnicity of the candidates. To address this problem, we use algorithmic coding to determine the gender of nearly every candidate (categorised as 'woman' or 'man') with the 'genderizer' package in R. Similarly, we use the 'wru' package in R to code race and ethnicity. The 'wru' package in R relies on US Census data to generate continuous probabilities indicating the likelihood that an individual with a specific name is white, Black, Hispanic, AAPI, Native American, multiracial, or other. This function is configured to consider the location of each candidate in California, taking into account the specific county where the individual is running for office (e.g., the probability that the last name 'Jefferson' belongs to a Black individual is higher in Los Angeles than in Tuolumne County). Due to the prevalence of whites in both the US Census and California, this measure may underestimate the likelihood that an individual is non-white, particularly for African Americans.

We also use the CEDA data to analyse the individual occupations of nearly 99,000 candidates on the ballot for local election in California. In local elections in California, all candidates are asked to provide a 'ballot designation': a brief (50 characters or less) description of their occupation, which is listed on the ballot next to their name. As an initial occupational coding, we manually coded each candidate's ballot designation into 540 categories that match the US Census's Occupational Categories. For example, we would classify someone who lists their job as 'Barber' as the Census Occupational Category of 4500: Barbers.

We then group these 540 categories into ten larger sectors and industries, such as business, education, health, and construction. Here, the 'Barber' category is grouped in the 'Personal Care' category, which includes such other occupations as 'Embalmers', 'Baggage Porters', and 'Fitness Instructors'. These are choices that are informed by the Census Bureau's designation of occupations, industries, and status. This allows us to compare the percentage of the *general population* in a given industry (using the US Census data for California) to the percentage of *political candidates* in said industry (using the

CEDA data) to the percentage of *election winners* in said industry. At some points in our analysis, we also create a series of occupational 'dummy' categories that allow for an inclusive coding of anyone who lists any job in that occupation.

We provide an initial view of what this data looks like in Figure 2, which presents the share of candidates who are women for each of the major race and ethnic groups in our data: Asian Americans/Pacific Islander, Black, Hispanic, and white. The figure also provides a view of the number of women candidates in our dataset. As the figure shows, the share of women in each occupation *does* vary some across racial and ethnic groups, but at no point do women from any racial or ethnic group cross more than half of any occupational category among our candidates. Because gender segregation by occupation is much starker than racial segregation by occupation, going forward, we do not break our results down by race and ethnicity, but as we know so little about the descriptive representation of women and minorities at the local level, we provide a breakdown by gender and race here. Moving forward in our analysis, we large focus on gender and occupation, leaving questions of race and ethnicity to future work.

By combining the Census with the CEDA dataset, we can examine three full populations: the entire population in the state of California, all of the candidates for local office, and all of the candidates who win local office. At the end of this section, we begin our analyses by comparing the general population to candidates and winners to see who opts into and out of politics by gender and occupation.

Emerge

To understand how potential candidates might make these decisions, we also incorporate data from two years of candidate trainings in California run by a national organisation, Emerge America, which trains progressive women to run for office. We also undertook unstructured interviews with some of the consultants and candidates involved, and conducted a national survey of the organisation's 2,083 alumnae for more details, see Bernhard, Shames, and Teele (2021) and Shames, Bernhard, Holman, and Teele (2020). This approach allows us to witness women in the process of deciding whether to run for political office. Notably, only 51 per cent of the participating women ultimately choose to pursue political office, despite undergoing months of training and incurring substantial costs. This variation in decision-making among women is crucial to understanding the dynamics involved.

The training sessions we observed took place during the 2014–2015 and 2015–2016 cohort years, each consisting of approximately 45 women with diverse backgrounds in terms of ethnicity, sexual orientation, socioeconomic

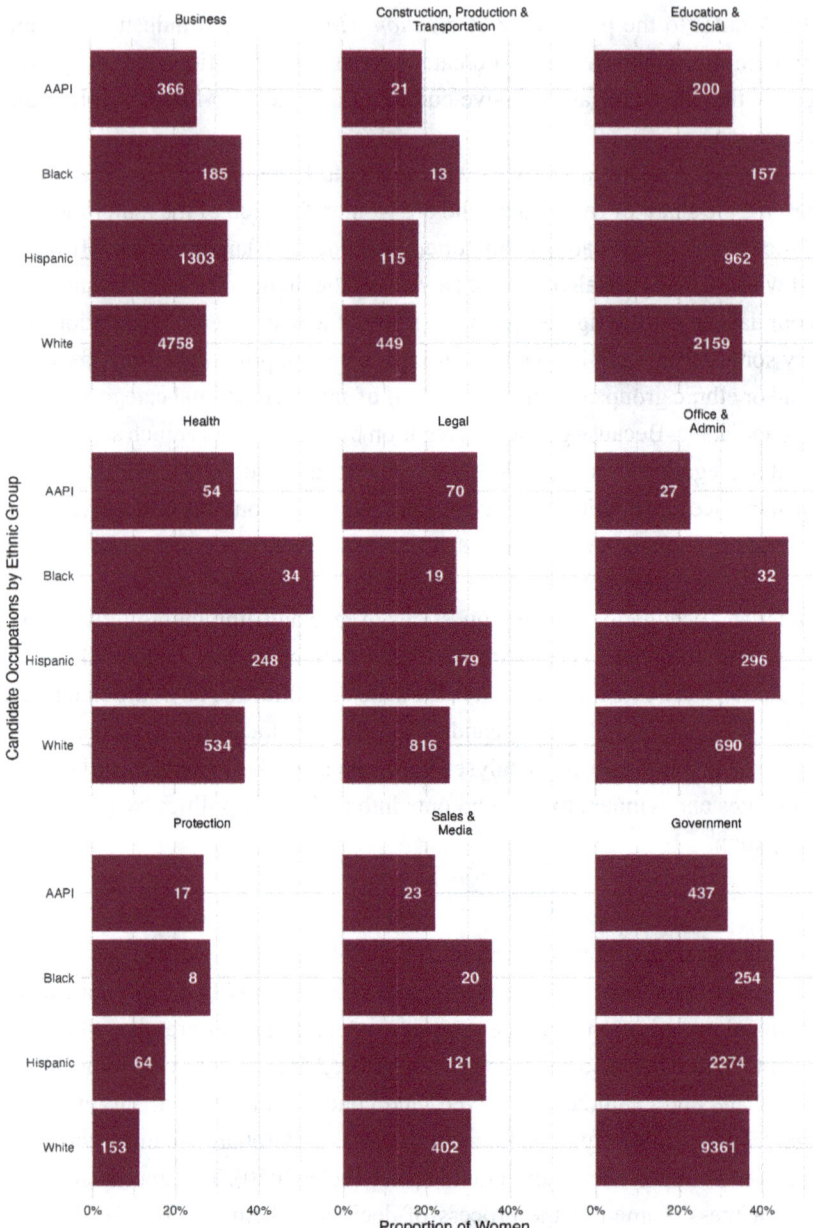

Figure 2 Women across racial groups are segregated like the general population. As with the general population, occupational gender segregation is much more dramatic than ethnic segregation by occupation. Number of women candidates per sector and racial/ethnic group is shown in white font in each bar.

status, age, and prior political experience. While the three programme staff remained constant across both cohorts, there was considerable demographic diversity in the characteristics of the pools of political consultants and participants. Ten per cent of participants identified as Asian American and Pacific Islander, 20 per cent as Black or African American, 36 per cent as Non-Hispanic White, 23 per cent as Hispanic/Latina, and 11 per cent as Other or Multiracial. Eighty-seven per cent also identified as straight, 10 per cent as LGBTQ, and 3 per cent declined to say or were missing data. Their ages spanned from 31 to 64 (median 41).[12] Finally, 45 per cent were single or divorced, 52 per cent married or partnered, and 3 per cent declined to say or were missing data (for more on why this might matter, see Bernhard et al., 2018).

Although the specific training topics varied slightly each year, the sessions generally covered public speaking, media, and messaging; fundraising; networking and endorsements; campaign strategy; field operations; ethics; and considerations of diversity. A typical training day involved workshops focusing on one of these topics, with two to three sets of consultants delivering presentations, alumnae providing the 'elected' graduates' perspective, and interactive activities such as practice pitches and fundraising call simulations. Trainees engaged in Q&A sessions during each session and socialised during meals and networking events.

The Emerge programme, hosted annually, is demanding, spanning six months and incorporating around 70 hours of training, primarily through full weekend workshops.[13] The daily schedule is also demanding, with Saturday training sessions often extending from 9 AM to 9 PM, excluding informal socialising afterward. Weekend 'boot-camps' include evening events for networking and practicing fundraising skills.

Our informal interviews with trainees occurred during breaks or over meals, while more formal interviews with programme staff were typically scheduled in advance and often conducted over the phone. After the second programme year in May 2016, we collaborated with the organisation to administer a national survey to all alumnae, consisting of approximately 20 minutes of questions covering demographics, detailed quantitative measures of potential barriers to office (such as childcare responsibilities), and open-ended inquiries about their

---

[12] A number of individuals appeared older or younger but were missing data; 27 individuals did not provide their ages, but all had to be at least 18 to participate in the training

[13] The application process for prospective candidates involves applying in October, receiving acceptance notifications in November, participating in training from December to May, and concluding with a graduation ceremony in June.

decision-making process regarding running for office (for more information, see Bernhard et al., 2018; Shames et al., 2020).

Survey and Experimental Data

Our final dataset is derived from surveys we have run asking people about their perceptions of various jobs and elected offices. We provide details on the general data collection process here and describe questions in more detail in each section before we present the results.

In our online survey, run through the LUCID Fulcrum platform, we asked 1,579 Americans a variety of questions about occupations (described below), offices (described in Section 4), and the electability of people from different occupations for a variety of local offices (also discussed in Section 6).[14] The study sample was designed to be approximately representative of the US population on gender and race/ethnicity: 50.6 per cent of respondents were women and 0.3 per cent selected other or declined to state. Approximately 72 per cent identified as white, 12 per cent as Black, 5 per cent as AAPI, 10 per cent as Native American, multiracial, or other, and 0.3 per cent declined to answer.

Drawing on work by Valentino (2021) and measures regularly asked on the General Social Survey, we asked respondents the following question as a measure of *occupational prestige*:

> Where would you place each occupation in terms of its social standing? Please select 9 if you think that occupation has the highest possible social standing. Select 1 if you think it has the lowest possible social standing. If it belongs somewhere in between, just select the level that matches the social standing of the occupation.

Respondents rated 10 of the same Census list of 540 occupations we described in the last section. This means we have ratings of hundreds of different occupations, from 'Airplane Mechanics' to 'Farm Laborers' to 'Yarn Spinners'.

Then, drawing on work by Bittner and Goodyear-Grant (2017) and Kreitzer and Watts (2018), we asked the respondents to assess the same ten randomly chosen occupations on their perceived *femininity* using the following scale:

---

[14] LUCID Fulcrum pulls survey respondents from a wide set of online platforms of survey takers, with more than 2 million people coming across the platform in any day. As a result of the large number of participants, the Fulcrum platform can provide a sample that uses quotas to benchmark against a representative population of US residents. We fielded our survey in February 2024. The survey received human subjects approval from the University of Houston's Institutional Review Board, No. 00004510.

> Some occupations in society are seen as more feminine, while others are seen as more masculine. Below you will find a continuum that goes from left to right. We would like you to place each occupation somewhere along this scale: the far left of the scale reflects an occupation that you feel is 100% masculine, while the far right of the scale reflects an occupation that you feel is 100% feminine. Where would you place this occupation on this continuum? (0–100, where 0 represents occupations that are 100% masculine and 100 represents occupations that are 100% feminine).

Respondents were randomly assigned to either rate the prestige of the jobs first, or the femininity of the jobs first. We did not see any clear effect of question order, so we simply use all the data without a fixed effect for question order.

Taken together, these datasets allow us to describe at a fine-grained level who runs for and wins office as a function of their gender and occupation.

3 Gendered Occupational Segregation Shapes Who Runs and Wins Local Office

> All of the strong character traits
> [for politics] are masculine. That's
> where we get stuck.
>
> *– H., Commission Chairwoman*

Our first empirical section answers a key question: compared to the general population, who runs for office and who wins? The data and methodological challenges we outline in Section 2 mean that it has been hard to study patterns of gendered occupations and candidate emergence at the local level; we offer new data to fill this gap. We begin by reviewing existing work on how gender shapes political ambition, and then how occupation shapes candidate emergence. Within each of those sections, we provide a view of the distribution of political candidates by gender and professional sector to see how these two factors shape who runs and who wins.

Gender and Ambition

From girls in elementary school to college students to 'ordinary women' to women with elite backgrounds, women are less interested in a political career, in running for office, or in holding office (Bernhard et al., 2021; Bos et al., 2021; Crowder-Meyer, 2020; Schneider et al., 2016; Wolbrecht & Campbell, 2007). The gap between women and men in interest in political office can be traced to a wide set of causes, including gender role socialisation, risk and conflict avoidance, gender biases of voters and political leaders, and the patriarchal and gendered nature of political opportunity.

As we discussed in Section 1, socialised gender roles push women towards communal goals and activities—ones that serve others and express care and concern—and men towards agentic goals and activities – ones that primarily serve the individual and express decisiveness and independence. Because political office is seen as fulfilling agentic roles (Okafor, 2017; Rudman & Phelan, 2008; Schneider et al., 2022) and requiring agentic skills (Holman et al., 2022; Sweet-Cushman, 2020a, 2021), women's gender socialisation pushes them towards activities like non-profit leadership and volunteering over seeking political office. And voters, who have been socialised in the same system, hold women seeking political office to particularly high standards because their gender is *incongruent with* seeking a political leadership role.

The association of men with leadership roles leads to a mismatch between views of the skills and expertise that women have and our expectations for our leaders. This 'double-bind' is particularly powerful for women seeking political roles: women politicians lose the positive attributes women are generally stereotyped as having, like warmth and empathy, but don't gain the positive attributes men are stereotyped as having, like assertiveness and confidence (N. M. Bauer, 2020a; Schneider & Bos, 2014). As a result, women must engage in work to demonstrate they are capable of leadership (being strong leaders, for example), and simultaneously avoid giving voters the idea that they are not capable of doing work that women should be good at, such as working with others. One consequence of this is that women often seek out offices where the expectations of 'masculine' behaviour are lower, such as school boards, city clerks, and secretary of education (Anzia, 2022; Crowder-Meyer, 2013; Fox & Oxley, 2003).

Women are also excluded from many of the important political networks that guide recruitment into political office and facilitate access to resources necessary to succeed as a political candidate (Barber et al., 2016; Crowder-Meyer, 2013; Thomsen & Sanders, 2020). The adage that 'it's not what you know, it's who you know' is particularly true in local politics, where political networks are insular and dependent on the activities of central leaders like political party chairs (Butler & Preece, 2016; Crowder-Meyer, 2013). As a result, women must be 'self-starters' to run for office: seeking opportunities without strong encouragement from others. This entrepreneurial spirit—and the ability to access resources needed to run—is associated with agentic traits, career choices, and risk tolerance, leading to gender gaps in who is willing to engage in such activities (Sánchez & Licciardello, 2012; Thébaud, 2010, 2015). One consistent result is that women are less likely to sort into careers that require entrepreneurial effort or to seek out local political opportunities.

Women Run for Offices That They Can Win

Running for office is inherently risky: one is spending time, money, family resources, connections, and personal capital on an outcome that is rarely guaranteed. Women avoid risk and conflict generally and electoral conflict specifically (Friesen & Holman, 2022; Kanthak & Woon, 2015; Preece & Stoddard, 2015; Schneider et al., 2016),[15] making political ambition particularly unlikely for women. Given that these risk and conflict preferences also shape individual choices about their careers and their positions within occupations (Canary, Cunningham, & Cody, 1988; Thébaud, 2010) those individuals who select careers with few conflicts might also be less interested in running for office. For example, someone might seek out a teaching career because the job is seen as stable, with reliable health insurance and retirement income; that same person may be less interested in running for office because they see it as a risky enterprise.

Women, particularly politically ambitious women, are also highly rational political actors. Because women who run for office are interested in winning, they run where they believe that they will be able to win (Anzia & Bernhard, 2022; Bernhard et al., 2021; Ondercin, 2022; Shames et al., 2020). For example, Ondercin (2022) finds that women running for Congressional offices in the United States are much more likely to emerge as candidates when the district's characteristics have helped women get elected in the past. Some of this relates directly to women's perceptions that the political system is biased against women generally (N. M. Bauer, 2020b; Teele, Kalla, & Rosenbluth, 2018); as a result, women often wait until they are more qualified to overcome any potential biases (Fulton et al., 2006; Kanthak & Woon, 2015; Shames et al., 2020).

Another consequence of women's strategic activity is that women often run for specific offices where they believe they are more likely to be elected, such as school board and city clerk (Anzia & Bernhard, 2022; Crowder-Meyer et al., 2015; Fox & Oxley, 2004) and even highly accomplished women do not believe they are qualified to run for political office. These are also self-reinforcing systems, where women see more women in offices like school board and then run for those specific offices because the office is seen as better aligning with women's goals. These patterns are also different across gender

---

[15] However, much of this work is based on the experiences of white women and may not apply to women of colour (Friesen & Holman, 2022; Holman, 2016a; Silva & Skulley, 2019).

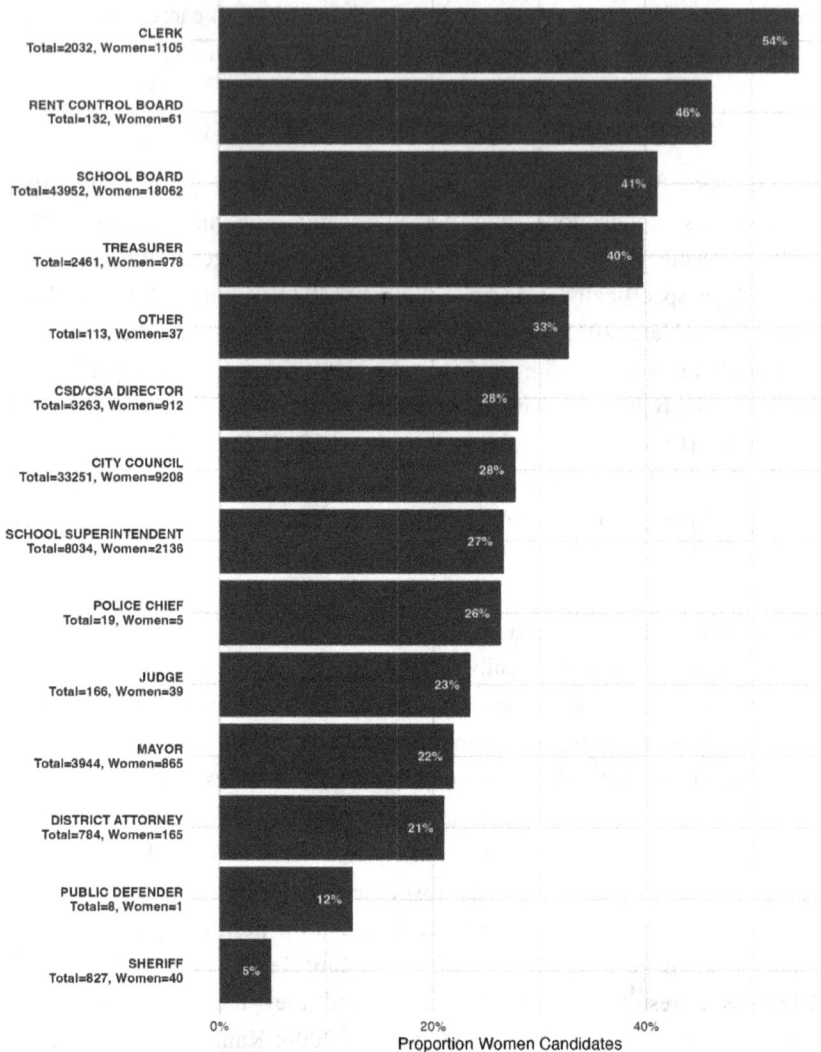

Figure 3 The share of women candidates varies across different local offices. As with occupations, women are much more likely to run for some offices than others. CEDA data.

and race, so the factors that shape white women's emergence as candidates do not necessarily apply to women of colour (Fraga, Gonzalez Juenke, & Shah, 2020; Holman, 2016a; Silva & Skulley, 2019).

Our observational data is consistent with these predictions: as Figure 3 shows, women are much more likely to run for some offices than others. The places where women run at higher levels are consistent with stereotypes about women's gender roles, like clerk and school board, and much less likely to run for offices inconsistent with those roles, like sheriff and police chief.

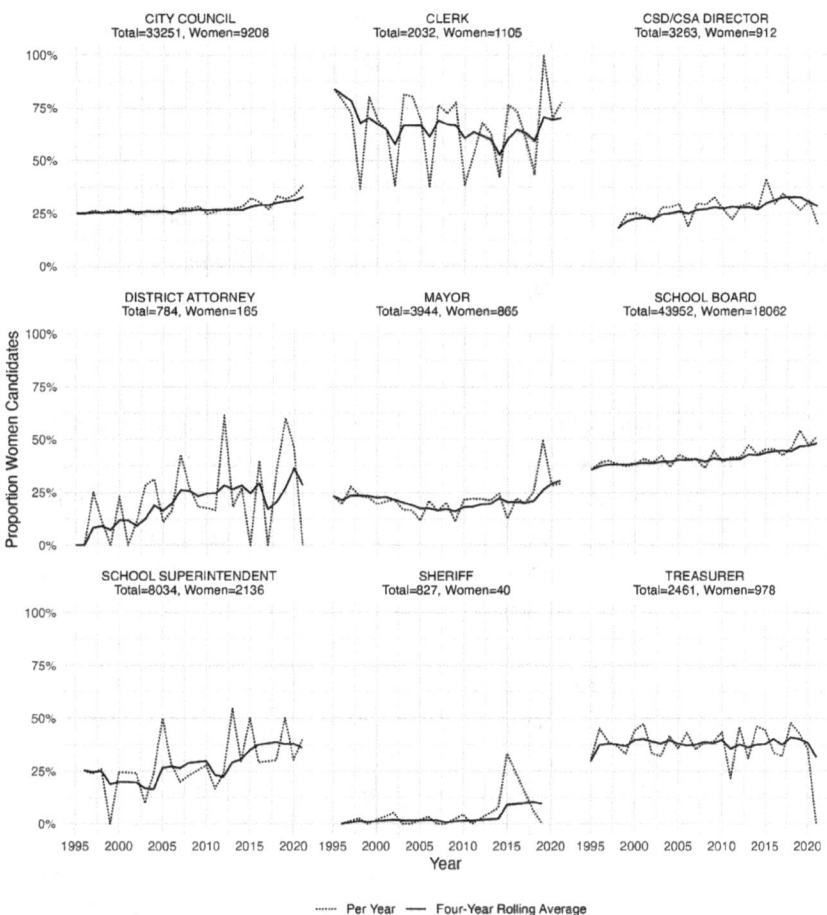

Figure 4 The share of women as candidates over time by local office. The number of women candidates has slightly increased over time, but only in some offices. CEDA data.

Moreover, despite rhetoric about women's progress towards equality in society (and women's increased educational attainment and work outside the home), the share of women candidates has stayed the share of women candidates has stayed constant or only slightly increased over the twenty-six years for which we have data, as shown in Figure 4. Notably, for almost all offices, the variation in the percentage of candidates for that office who are women is much larger *across* offices than *within* offices over time.

We can see that there is only a slight increase over time in the number of women running for city council, community services director, mayor, and sheriff. There are more substantial increases in the number of women running for district attorney, school board, and school superintendent. There is little to no increase, or even a decrease, in the number of women running for clerk and treasurer. In the earliest years of the data, women tended to run in high numbers only for feminine-stereotyped roles like clerk and school board, but as time has gone on, more women have acquired the skills, networks, and resources to run for positions like district attorney. And while the absolute numbers are still very low, we can start to see a measurable number of women running for extremely masculine-stereotyped roles like sheriff, where previously there were zero women candidates in many years (for discussion see Farris & Holman, 2024).

Voting and Elections in Local Politics

While much of what we know about gender and politics has focused on national or state politics, we can learn from the scholarship on voting and elections in local politics to understand women's exclusion. What we *do* know is that low information about local elections represents one important obstacle to women's ability to access political office. Broadly, voters are often uninformed about local politics, with few opportunities to remedy their lack of information (Bernhard & Freeder, 2020; de Benedictis-Kessner, 2017; Schaffner & Streb, 2002; Trounstine, 2013). This is particularly true when elections are local elections where election dates are more likely to be 'off-cycle' (that is, not aligned with Congressional or presidential elections), non-partisan, and for more obscure offices like sheriff and city clerk (Crowder-Meyer et al., 2015; de Benedictis-Kessner, 2017; Farris & Holman, 2023a).

There is reason to believe that the gender stereotypes that we discuss in Sections 1 and 2 would apply more strongly at the local level. The little information that voters have about local offices leads to the reliance on information shortcuts—cues—that replace more complete information (Crowder-Meyer, Gadarian, & Trounstine, 2019; Holman, Merolla, & Zechmeister, 2017; Kreiss, Lawrence, & McGregor, 2020; McDermott & Panagopoulos, 2015). Gender is one of the most central and available information shortcuts available to voters, particularly in the context of non-partisan elections (Badas & Stauffer, 2023).

Occupation and Candidate Emergence

What about the occupations of candidates? While the influence of one's job on one's status, life expectancy, earnings, and experiences are well documented (i.e., Friedman & Laurison, 2019), less is known about how occupation interacts with gender to shape pathways to and experiences of political candidacy. Work on political class as measured by occupation often focuses on how those from blue-collar backgrounds (such as coming from unions or jobs that require physical labour like agricultural work) behave in political office (Barnes & Holman, 2018, 2020b; J. H. Kim, Kuk, & Kweon, 2024), or the sorts of criteria voters use to evaluate candidates, including their occupations and military service (Atkeson & Hamel, 2020; Coffé & Theiss-Morse, 2016; Kirkland, 2020; McDermott, 2005; McDermott & Panagopoulos, 2015; Mechtel, 2014).[16] But while scholarship explores how employment shapes political participation (for example, see Aalen et al., 2018; Greenberg, Grunberg, & Daniel, 1996; Iversen & Rosenbluth, 2008; Kjelsrud & Kotsadam, 2023; Schlozman, Burns, & Verba, 1999), very little explores the effects of either specific occupations on political engagement or how occupations might affect candidate emergence specifically. While no single existing theory exists as to why some professions might be more likely to select into and out of politics, we briefly review the most relevant work below.

Occupational Prestige, Class, and Wealth

Why might occupation matter to voters? Most obviously, it matters because voters want candidates to be competent to handle the 'portfolios' of their offices. For instance, voters see candidates with business backgrounds as better equipped to handle economic issues, and those with education backgrounds, human services issues (Campbell & Cowley, 2014; Coffé & Theiss-Morse, 2016); voters also see working-class women as particularly unsuited for political office (HJ. Kim & Kweon, 2024). Perhaps because this has seemed like such a no-brainer, there is surprisingly little work directly exploring how specific candidate occupations shape voting, though a large body of work does exist that explores how *much* occupational background matters to voters at the ballot box, for example, due to its use as a heuristic in low-information elections (McDermott, 2005; Mechtel, 2014). Instead, candidate occupation frequently operates 'invisibly' in studies of elections, serving as a control variable when political scientists can get such data (e.g., Anzia & Bernhard, 2022).

Occupations also might matter to voting in ways beyond the issue or domain competence they signal. Occupational prestige shapes interpersonal relationships, political attitudes, and social power as it 'explicitly represents social standing' (Fujishiro et al., 2010, 2100). Because occupational prestige shapes so many components of social exchanges, it also links to individual and group-based outcomes like civic participation, marriage, and health

---

[16] Of course, some of the most active strands of research on political economy focus on the effects of occupation on political attitudes and voting: for instance, antipathy towards immigration as a function of economic vulnerability (van Setten, Scheepers, & Lubbers, 2017), or the relationship between class mobility and preferences for redistribution (Alesina, Stantcheva, & Teso, 2018). New work, like that by van Staalduinen & Zollinger (2023), even explores the gendered dimensions of these trends.

(Fujishiro et al., 2010; Kalmijn, 1994; Kitschelt & Rehm, 2014; Sobel, 1993). While higher occupational prestige is associated with higher pay and more education or training requirements, these materialistic characteristics do not entirely explain an occupation's prestige. Instead, 'the typical sex or race of a class of jobs in workplaces becomes a fundamental aspect of the jobs, influencing the work done as well as the organisational evaluation of the worth of the work' (Tomaskovic-Devey, 2019, p. 6). Previous work suggests more feminine jobs are seen as less prestigious jobs, including over time: as women become the majority of workers in a previously male-dominated occupation, that occupation is then seen as less prestigious (Busch, 2020; Levanon, England, & Allison, 2009).

Yet even as political scientists have implicitly focused on occupational prestige (Barnes & Holman, 2023; O'Grady, 2019) or the role of specific occupations (Bonica, 2020; Kirkland, 2020), we know much less about how occupational prestige and perceptions of occupation as feminine influence political ambition and candidate success. Interestingly, in Figure 5, we see surprisingly little relationship between perceptions of how female-dominated and how prestigious an occupation is. (We will come back to the issue of occupational prestige in Section 4 when we look to see how real elections play out.) For instance, telemarketers are rated as the lowest prestige job in the dataset, but the perceived gender balance is nearly equal at 51 out of 100 on the masculine-feminine scale. Aircraft pilots and nurse practitioners are rated near the top for prestige, but pilots are masculine-coded (33 out of 100) and nurses, feminine-coded (74 out of 100).

One reason we may not see a stronger relationship between prestige and masculinity here is because the Census occupations that respondents rated are very specific. For instance, nurse practitioners, nurse midwives, nurse anaesthetists, registered nurses, and vocational nurses are all separate categories. So even though each occupation is rated approximately thirty times (by thirty respondents), respondents may have quite a bit of uncertainty about how prestigious these specific occupations are relative to one another.

Class is separate from (but directly related to) perceptions of occupational prestige. While scholars have extensively debated the ways and means of measuring class (A. K. Cohen & Hodges, 1963; Friedman & Laurison, 2019; Friedman, Laurison, & Miles, 2015; Rubin & Rubin, 1987), many researchers focus on occupational-based measures (O'Grady, 2019), including identifying jobs that do not require a college degree as working class and focusing on 'blue-collar' and 'pink-collar' occupational classifications (Barnes, Beall, & Holman, 2021; Barnes & Holman, 2023; Mastracci, 2004; Norris & Lovenduski, 1995; Royster, 2003). Despite class

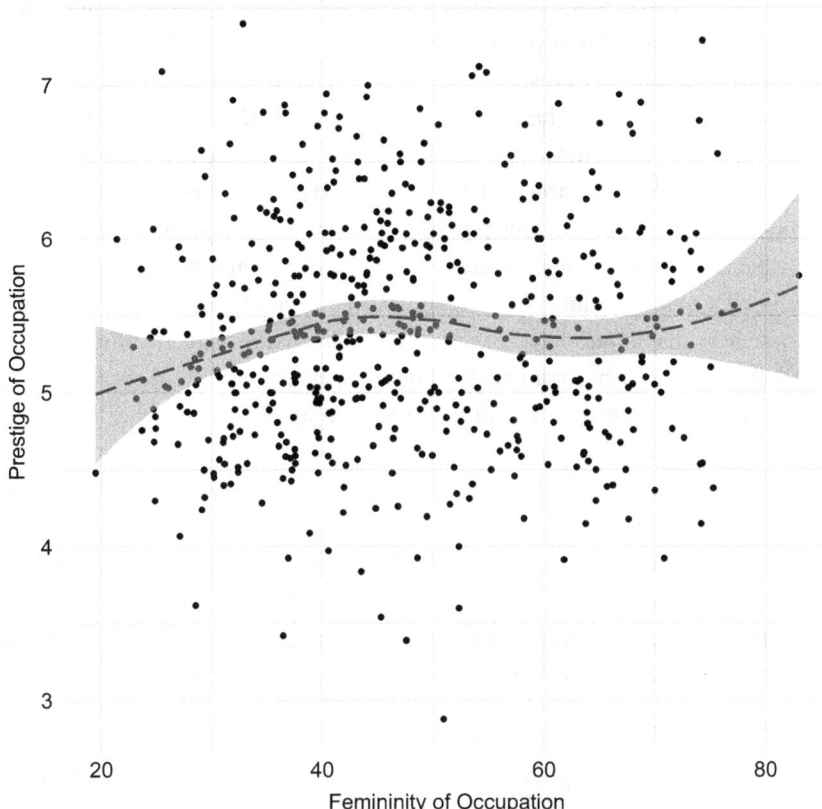

Figure 5 Perceived occupation femininity and prestige do not appear to be closely related. 540 Census occupations were rated on both dimensions by survey respondents.

shaping the preferences and behaviours of candidates and those elected to political office (Barnes, Kerevel, & Saxton, 2023; Grumbach, 2015; J. H. Kim, Kuk, & Kweon, 2024), evaluations of class advance an implicitly gendered definition of what it means to be a member of the working class (Carnes, 2018), a point discussed in detail by Barnes et al. (2021). And, evaluations of women's representation have largely ignored class, despite discussions of women's policymaking preferences being deeply rooted in the feminisation of poverty (Clayton & Zetterberg, 2018; Holman, 2014, 2015). Childs and Hughes (2018) and R. Murray (2023) offer two exceptions, exploring the extent to which elite and upper-caste women make up representative bodies around the world. Another exception is Campbell & Cowley (2014), who find that voters are turned off by ultra-wealthy candidates. Yet here, too, we know little about the connection between class and candidate emergence, beyond recognising that class and its correlates, like wealth and education, strongly predict who holds power in systems around the world.

Finally, occupational prestige is not only linked to class but wealth. There is of course an enormous body of work on the influence of money in politics (e.g., Gilens, 2012; Winters, 2011), with a smaller subset focusing on individual and household wealth (Carnes, 2018; Gilens, 2012), including on gender (e.g., Bernhard et al., 2024). For our purposes, we are less interested in the material aspects of occupations (although they are clearly important to shaping an individual's access to the resources necessary to run office); instead, we simply note here that in our data, we cannot disentangle the 'effects' of wealth (or class) from those of occupation. We hope that future work will explore these distinctions, for instance by finding ways to hold wealth constant while varying occupational prestige.

Drawing these bodies of literature together, we argue that one important and understudied set of factors is how gender and occupation influence who chooses to run for office and who is selected by voters. In the next section, we test this argument by analysing the shifts in the gender and occupation makeup of each group, starting with the general population and then looking at candidates and election winners.

From Population to Candidates to Leaders: Candidate Emergence by Occupation and Gender

So, who runs and who wins? In the top pane of Figure 6, we show the dramatic patterns of selection into (or out of) politics by industry. Some sectors like construction represent a large part of the workforce (22 per cent) but tend to produce very few candidates for office (just 5 per cent of candidates and 6 per cent of winners). Other industries like education, law, and protection produce many more candidates than their share of the population. The ratio of the population to candidates and winners here is meaningful: for the population, there are *more than five times* the number of lawyers in the candidate pool as there are in the general population, and *three times* the number of businesspeople. In comparison, office workers and construction workers make up just *one-fifth* of the share of candidates relative to their share of the general population. Alexandria Ocasio-Cortez's career as a bartender before running for Congress stands out here: while food service workers make up more than 5 per cent of workers, they are only 0.03 per cent of candidates and 0.02 per cent of elected leaders. This is notable, because, as Rep Ocasio-Cortez noted on Twitter: 'Bartending + waitressing (especially in NYC) means you talk to 1000s of people over the years. Forces you to get great at reading people + hones a razor-sharp BS detector.'

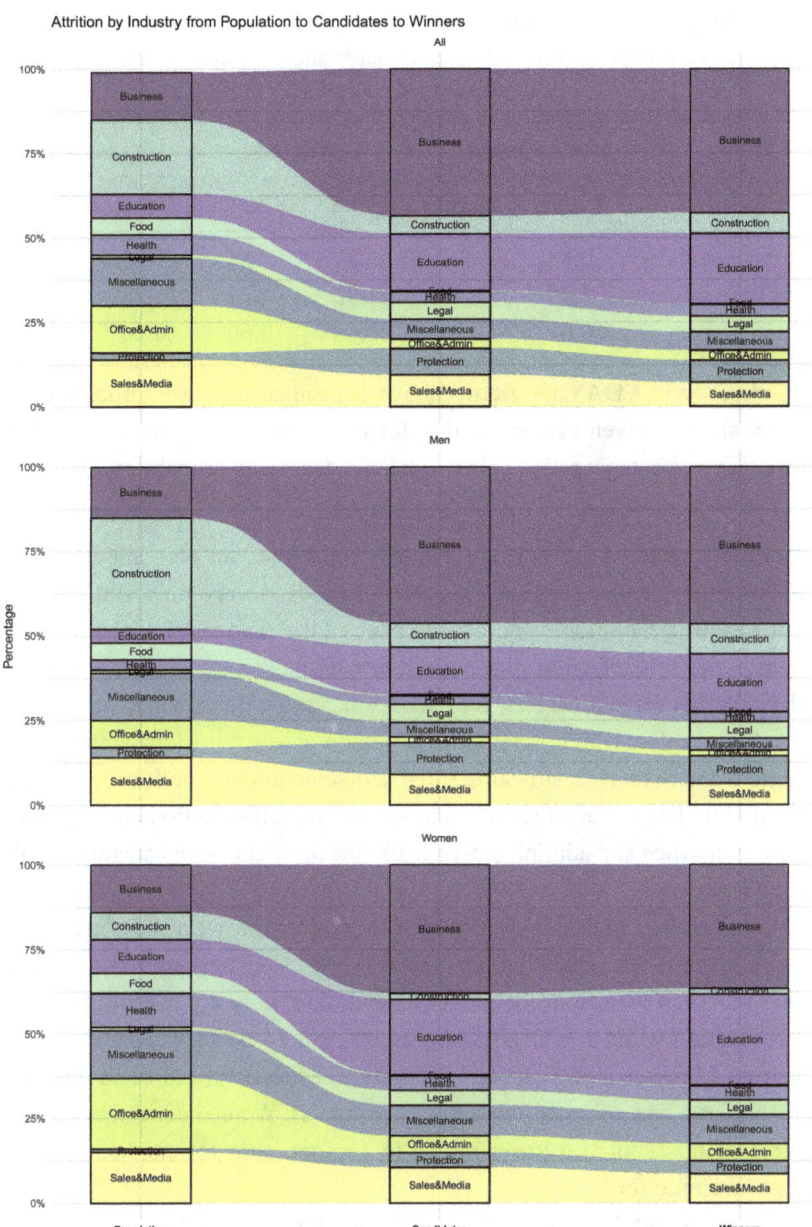

Figure 6 Business and education are the largest categories among candidates and winners, but not among the population. Population data from the American Communities Survey for California; candidate and elected leaders data from CEDA database, coded by authors, and excludes incumbents.

Table 1 Men with feminine occupations and women and men with masculine occupations are overrepresented as candidates and winners, compared to their share of the population.

	Both Genders		Women		Men	
	Cand.	Winner	Cand.	Winner	Cand.	Winner
Feminine careers	0.84	1.01	0.77	0.88	1.23	1.45
Masculine careers	1.49	1.45	1.92	1.83	1.23	1.24
Neutral careers	0.61	0.51	0.68	0.60	0.56	0.44

US Census and CEDA data. Ratios above 1 mean an increased probability of individuals in a given career running for or winning office relative to their population percentage; ratios below 1 mean a decreased probability.

But these patterns are not just about occupations, but also about gender. We know that gender segregation of occupations is very powerful and this reveals itself in the middle and bottom pane of the figure. Among men, there is substantial self-selection into politics among those in business, education, and protection-related careers, and substantial self-selection out of those in construction roles, which is the most common category of jobs among men. Among women, there is still substantial self-selection into politics from business, slightly less so for education, and substantial self-selection out of politics for those in office and administrative work (the most common category of jobs among women).

Education also stands out for both men and women. As we discuss in detail in Section 6, men from education backgrounds self-select into politics at a much higher rate than we see in the general population: only 4 per cent of men in the population work in education, but more than 14 per cent of male candidates and 17 per cent of male winners work in education (a three-to-one ratio for candidates and a four-to-one ratio for winners). Women educators are also overrepresented, but at a lower rate: a two-to-one ratio for candidates and a five-to-two ratio for winners.

We also present this data within broader feminine and masculine categories in Table 1. Here, we focus on the difference in the population share and the share of candidates and winners within each gender. Feminine occupations are those like education and office administration where women make up more than 60 per cent of the workforce in the occupation; masculine occupations follow as occupations dominated by men (Barnes & Holman, 2020a). We also include a 'neutral' category that includes occupational categories like sales and food preparation, where women and men make up similar portions of the occupation.

How does the representation of feminine, masculine, and neutral occupations in the population compare to candidates and elected representatives? In Table 1, a number under one indicates that the group is better represented in the general population than among candidates and winners. A number over one means that the group is better represented among candidates or winners than in the general population. For example, when we look at feminine careers for all candidates (first row and column of data), the 0.84 figure means that for every ten people in the general population who have a feminine occupation, roughly eight people with feminine occupations become candidates—and then ten will become winners (1.01), meaning that candidates from feminine careers win at higher rates than they appear as candidates. In comparison, the ratio of 1.49 for masculine careers and candidates (column one, row two) indicates that for every ten people in the general population with a masculine career, there are nearly fifteen (1.49) candidates and fifteen (1.45) winners.

Three patterns stand out in Table 1. We start with the finding that women with feminine careers (row one) are underrepresented in political office, while men from feminine occupations are overrepresented compared to their share of the population. Both men and women from feminine careers are better represented among winners than among candidates, but even voter preferences for women from feminine backgrounds do not overcome the supply issue. Second, the most reliably overrepresented group are masculine careers. This is especially true for women from masculine careers, where women from masculine occupations are nearly twice as likely to enter as the share of candidates as compared to their share in the population. And, third, while gender-neutral occupations make up more than 20 per cent of those in the workforce, this group selects *out of* politics and voters are less likely to select them compared to their share on the ballot.

In this section, we explored how gender and occupation shape engagement with the political system. We presented original data showing how well a broad set of occupations are descriptively represented among candidates and winners across all local political offices. Our analysis revealed that occupational gender segregation helps produce the occupational gender segregation of political candidates and winners. Moving forward, we consider how the alignment between the role of political leader and occupational femininity/masculinity shape who runs and wins local office.

4 Gender-Segregated Jobs Influence Perceived Occupational Femininity and Win Rates

> People like women in helping professions, not in traditional seats of power like CEO.
>
> – *S., City Councillor*

> If you're in any way male or masculine, you are advantaged in life and in politics.
>
> – *J., Political Consultant*

If you close your eyes and picture an elementary school teacher, what does that person look like? What about when you imagine a police officer? For most Americans, the image these occupations generate—a friendly woman working as an elementary school teacher, or a stern man working as a police officer—is heavily influenced by the gender distribution of those who work in the occupation. In fact, 80 per cent of elementary school teachers are women and 77 per cent of police officers are men.

The lives of women in advanced industrialised nations have changed enormously over the last half a century. Women have become nearly half of all wage earners and make up the majority of college graduates, new lawyers, and more than half of the managers of the US workforce. Yet, even as these dramatic shifts have occurred, the gender distribution of occupations has not shifted in large ways (Barnes & Holman, 2023; Guy & Newman, 2004; Roos & Reskin, 1984). For example, in 1990, 82.5 per cent of elementary school teachers were women. It is not just teachers and police officers, either: in 1991, 93 per cent of nurses and 8 per cent of engineers were women. In 2020, little had changed: women held 91 per cent of nursing jobs and 14 per cent of engineering positions. Nursing, teaching, law enforcement, and engineering are not anomalies: more than half of the workforce in the United States are employed in gender-segregated occupations (Busch, 2020). A full 53 per cent of women in the United States would have to shift into a currently male-dominated occupation to eliminate gender segregation in the workforce (Levanon & Grusky, 2016). Scholars note that the prospects of reducing the 'remarkable persistence' of gender segregation of occupations 'remain slim' (P. N. Cohen, 2013). The United States is not alone: while research on gendered segregation in occupations has often focused on the United States and Europe (Elsässer & Schäfer, 2023; Razzu & Singleton, 2018), recent work shows that gendered segregation in occupations and sectors is increasing in the developing world (Borrowman & Klasen, 2020).

Gendered segregation in occupations is rooted in women's exclusion from public spaces. Until the twentieth century, most women were confined to informal work, including full-time caretaking in the home, due to norms about women being more suited to the private/domestic sphere and men being more suited to the public sphere (Baker et al., 2010; Diekman & Goodfriend, 2006; Wolbrecht & Campbell, 2007). Broadly, these patterns may be understood as more or less direct forms of gender discrimination (Beller, 1982; Zellner, 1972), also called a 'demand-side' factor in women's labour force participation. The demand for women's caretaking work still persists today (Diekman et al., 2011).

Of course, there has always been substantial variation in women's labour force participation across households as a function of household wealth (and therefore its correlates, like race: see Sokoloff, 1992): wealthier households could afford to have women in non-paying work, or even purchase additional services like nannies and cooks, while poorer households often relied on women to work feminine-typed paying jobs (e.g., as nannies and cooks) to make ends meet. And, as hooks (2014) notes, women of colour have always worked outside the home in subjugated labour for white people.

These patterns endure even as norms about women's suitability for paying work have changed (Diekman & Eagly, 2000) in part because women continue to face structural challenges to work, especially related to motherhood (Calarco, 2024; Iversen & Rosenbluth, 2008). Women face more substantial career interruptions due to parenthood than men do, and once they become parents, expectations about caretaking are still higher than for men who become parents. One famous example of such burdens is the 'second shift' (Hochschild & Machung, 2012), wherein mothers come home from paying work (the first shift) to undertake unpaid domestic labour (the second shift). These expectations in turn keep women out of many 'greedy jobs' (jobs that demand a great deal of time and focus), such as doctor, lawyer, or politician (Goldin, 2021). As such, women may choose jobs that enable more flexibility or fewer penalties for undertaking caregiving work or taking time off for pregnancy and child rearing (Beller, 1982).

An additional reason patterns of occupational segregation persist is that members of groups internalise these gender norms. This is sometimes also called 'supply-side' segregation (Anker, 1997). Simply, many women derive more satisfaction from communally oriented jobs (e.g., teaching or healthcare) than agentic-oriented jobs (e.g., sales or law) (Evans & Diekman, 2009). This means that women sort into these jobs at higher rates even when expectations about caretaking at home or job 'greediness' are held constant. Indeed, Diekman and Goodfriend (2006) and Diekman et al. (2010) find that women are more likely to pursue STEM careers (masculine-typed jobs) when they are presented as being more communally oriented. Similarly, scholars have found that women are more likely to consider pursuing jobs in politics when they believe those jobs help others (Schneider et al., 2016).

The causes and consequences of this gendered occupational segregation have received much attention from researchers, with special attention paid to the ways that gender role theory contributes to these segregated patterns (Diekman et al., 2010; Eagly, Wood, & Diekman, 2000). We know much less about how gendered segregation of occupations influences the path to office. Researchers have shown that gender segregation of occupations shapes factors like policy outcomes (Barnes & Holman, 2023), political interests and career choices (Schneider & Bos, 2019), and political ambition (Schneider et al., 2016). And Oliver and Conroy (2018, 2020) show that masculinity plays an essential role in politics: masculine personality traits are associated with higher levels of feeling qualified for office, access to political recruitment, and progressive ambition. On the other hand, our work also finds that voters in California seem to prefer candidates more when they are described with feminine, collaborative leadership styles, rather than masculine, assertive leadership styles (Bernhard, 2022), but that the feminine advantage is particularly strong for candidates seeking offices like school board and city clerk (Anzia & Bernhard, 2022).

We argue that gender roles shape political office because most occupations are seen as gendered. That is, people do not see teachers or police officers or accountants as simply gender-neutral occupations, but are informed by the actual gender composition of these occupations. As such, teachers are seen as feminine and police officers are seen as masculine. After we demonstrate how these patterns map onto the actual gendered distribution of workers in the United States, we then show that these perceptions of the masculinity or femininity of an occupation predict who runs for and who wins office.

Perceptions of Masculinity, Femininity, and Occupational Gender Segregation

We expect that the public is aware of these long-term persistent patterns in occupational gender segregation. As a result, people will see occupations where there are more women as more feminine and individuals with those backgrounds will be disadvantaged when seeking political office. Here, we present the correspondence between perceptions of femininity (as measured in our survey, discussed in Section 2) and the share of women in those professions.

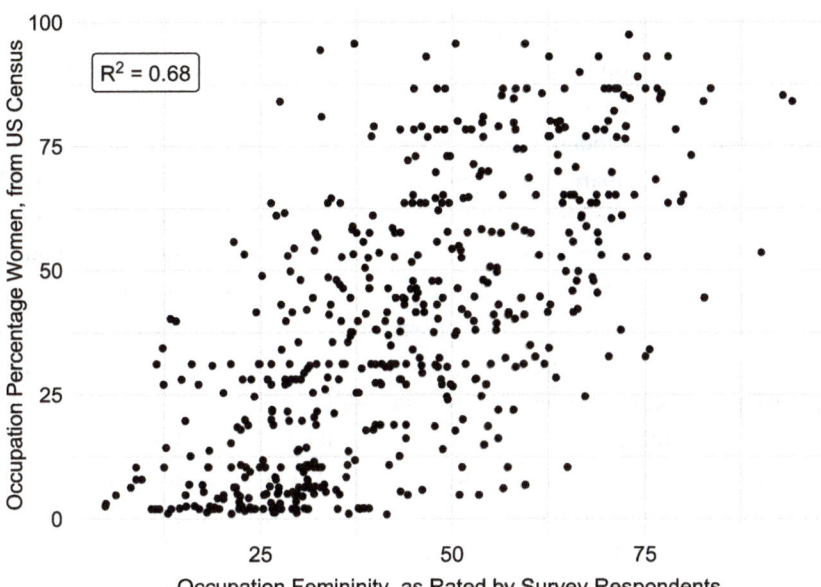

Figure 7 Survey respondents' perceptions of masculinity/femininity of an occupation closely track actual rates of women in those professions. Survey and US Census data.

As we expected, perceptions of the masculinity or femininity of an occupation closely track the actual numbers of women in those roles. Figure 7 shows the correlation between the percentage of women by occupation in the Census and the estimated femininity of each occupation from the survey data. Women make up 2.6 per cent of iron and steel workers, for instance, and this received the lowest femininity rating in our dataset, at 4.8/100. Conversely, hairstylists and nurse midwives had the highest femininity ratings, at 94.3 and 93.0 out of 100 respectively. Unsurprisingly, women compose 84.1 per cent and 85.3 per cent of those professions. In other words, although respondents certainly do not know the exact gender breakdown of a given profession, they can place gender-segregated jobs at either extreme and place unsegregated jobs in the middle of the range.[17]

Role Congruity, Femininity, and Elections

How does this sort of gendered occupational role congruity matter, though, for shaping who holds political office? Much scholarly attention has been paid to the association between gender and leadership, including work that

---

[17] While there is noise within these ratings, we do see that they vary by the gender composition of the occupation even within the same sector. For example, women hold two-thirds (66.7 per cent) of physician assistant positions and respondents assigned the occupation a femininity score of 76. Women are 48 per cent of dentists, and the respondents assigned that occupation a femininity score of 40.

we have done (Bernhard, 2022; Holman et al., 2022; Shames et al., 2020). Research reliably finds that individuals associate men and masculinity with leadership, particularly political leadership. For example, a meta-analysis of 69 different studies found consistently large correlations between masculinity and leadership (compared to femininity and leadership) (Koenig et al., 2011).[18]

We are interested in how people perceive individual occupations, rather than specific leadership roles. Recall that we expect that occupations seen as more feminine by the public will be less likely to run for office and to win an election. To test this argument, we examine the relationship between gender-occupation role congruity for candidates and winners in the CEDA data, showing whether and when role congruity correlates with political selection by gender. To do so, we assign the crowdsourced masculinity/femininity coding to the occupations listed by candidates in the CEDA data. For example, if a candidate listed their career as 'preschool teacher', we apply the femininity rating of 72.9 that corresponds to that occupation. We can then estimate the femininity rating for occupations held by men and women in the population; men and women running for office; and men and women who win elections.

We estimate the likelihood that any particular candidate wins an election by the perceived femininity of the occupation that any candidate lists on the ballot; we present the effect of femininity on the likelihood of winning in Figure 8. In the figure, we show the bivariate effect in the first line of the figure (i.e., what is the total effect of femininity on winning without controls), with county and year fixed effects in the second line of the figure; office fixed effects in the third line; controlling for the prestige of the occupation held by the candidate in the fourth line; and the effect for non-incumbents (plus fixed effects for county, year, and office) only in the final line.

Do voters prefer candidates with more feminine occupations when making a selection in a local election? Contrary to some earlier work suggesting femininity (in other forms) might harm candidates' chances, yes. Even with an exceedingly conservative estimation strategy of controlling for time, location, and office, we see a significant, positive effect of occupational femininity on the probability that a candidate will win an election. We continue to see an effect when we include or exclude incumbents in our models, suggesting that voters use occupational femininity as an information shortcut when making decisions about candidates. These effects are substantively large: in the most conservative regression, we would estimate that moving from a 0 (totally masculine job) to a 100 (totally feminine job) would improve a female candidate's chances of

---

[18] Notably, most of these studies focused on mid-level managers, which have a lower association with masculinity than high-level positions, and the association between masculinity and leadership appears to be diminishing over time (Koenig et al., 2011, pp. 2, 19).

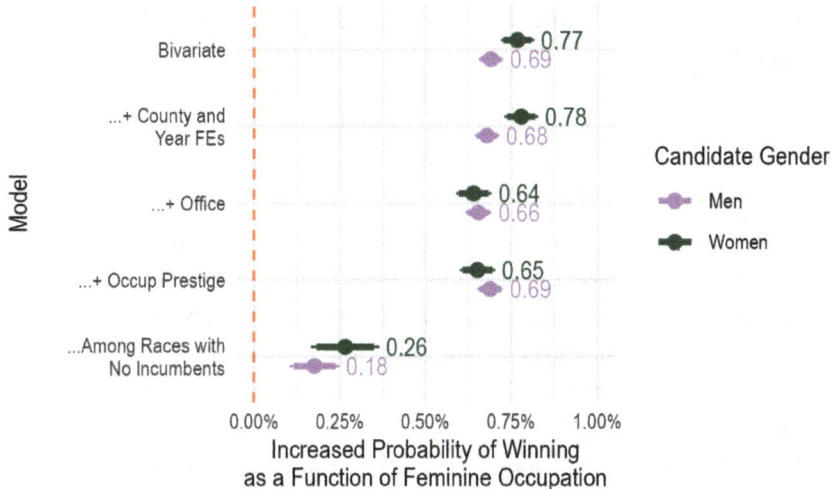

Figure 8 The more feminine the candidate's occupation, the more likely they are to win their election. This holds for both men and women candidates. CEDA and survey data.

winning by 26 per cent, and a male candidate's chances of winning by 18 per cent. These are big effects when many local elections feature multiple candidates and low-percentage individual vote shares as a result. However, as we'll return to in Section 6, there are good reasons not to over-interpret this finding, because the results look quite different across different offices!

In this section, we first demonstrated that the public generally sees occupations with more women as more feminine. In short, people pay attention to the distribution of men and women across occupations in the population. The historical 'stickiness' of gendered segregation into occupations probably contributes to this; for example, we see a stronger correlation between the share of women and perceptions of femininity for jobs where the gender distribution of the workforce has changed less over the last twenty years.

We then drew on work by Oliver and Conroy (2018, 2020) to argue that these perceptions of femininity shape who runs for office and who wins. We build on Oliver and Conroy's (2020) work by demonstrating that their findings about personality also apply to observational data about the occupations of individuals who run for and win local office. Because of the remarkable stickiness of gender role socialisation, the power of path dependency, and the role of factors as diverse as gender bias to role models to preferences for same-gender social networks, these gendered occupational segregation patterns are here to stay.

Yet contrary to some existing scholarship, we also found that having a feminine occupation may not harm candidates' chances, and could even help them win elections. In the next sections, we explore whether that is equally true for all offices.

5 It's Not What You Know, It's Who You Know: Why Business Leaders and Teachers Dominate Local Politics

In the past few sections, we have shown how two professions above all serve as a feeder for local politics: business and teaching. But why is that? Is it all about selection—for instance, that the types of people who go into business and education have personalities that make them a really good fit for politics—or is something else going on? Is it about skills, or networks? In this section, we delve deeper, trying to answer two main questions. First, what explains the dominance of these occupations in the candidate pool and in winning elections? Second, is the story that explains the dominance of business the same story that explains why teachers are motivated to run? In this section, we show that although the reasons these professions are prominent in local politics differ substantially from one another, both are still stories about organised interests. And because the two jobs that underlie these organised interests tend to be gender segregated (business still heavily dominated by men, and teaching, by women), so are our local politics.

The Dominance of Business in Local Politics

The very earliest studies of power in urban politics point to the centrality of business leaders in politics (Hunter, 1953; Lynd & Lynd, 1929). Subsequent central theories of urban politics point to businesses (particularly those involved in property development) as key power brokers (Molotch, 1976) and as a necessary component for local economic growth (Stone, 1989). In her investigation of the backgrounds of mayors in large cities, Kirkland (2021) finds that business leaders account for more than a third of candidates for office across fifty years: 'business owners and executives are extraordinarily well represented in American city halls.' The backgrounds of candidates shown in Figure 9 have a similar composition.

But why is business ownership such a common path for candidates in local politics? One answer lies in the nature of urban political finances under American federalism. Cities operate as agents of the state: that is, cities only legally exist because they are created by state governments. As a result, states can and do place a wide set of constraints on local governments, from restricting their funding sources to limiting their ability to make policy on issues as wide-ranging as minimum wage to plastic bag bans.

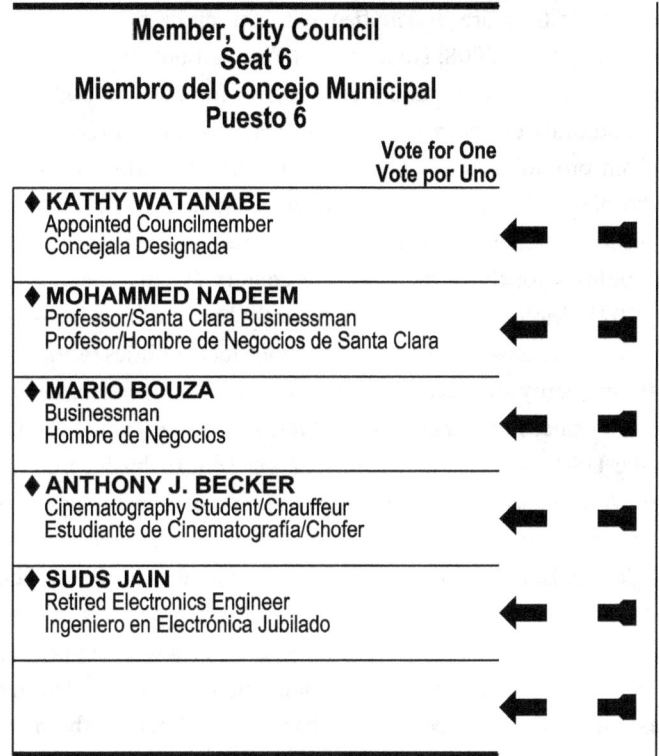

Figure 9 Business on the ballot. Sample ballot from Santa Clara County, CA.

Constraints on the sources, amounts, and spending choices greatly restrict the behaviour of city leaders. Cities are not economically independent: they have a small set of kinds of taxes they can apply (typically, property and some sales taxes but almost never income taxes), their tax rates on these items are often capped, and borrowing money is largely limited to capital projects and requires approval by voters or the state legislature (Y. Kim, 2019; Peck, 2012).[19]

Because of these restrictions, cities look to the kinds of revenue they can control: property taxes. The path to financial prosperity (or even financial survival) for cities starts with maintaining and increasing the value of property (Molotch, 1976; Peterson, 1981). Because residents can choose where they live and businesses can choose where to locate, cities are faced with the very real threat of high-income residents and powerful businesses simply moving

---

[19] Much of what cities have to spend is through intergovernmental transfers, where the state and federal governments give cities back some of the money that their residents paid in taxes. These funds can be unreliable; for example, when the federal government changes party control, this often means changes in the priorities of what gets funded for cities and how it gets funded.

to another city if they are dissatisfied with the city's policies or quality of life (Banzhaf & Walsh, 2008; Hirschman, 1970; Tiebout, 1956). Centring businesses in political decision-making thus allows for cities to both retain them in the city and draw on the resources that businesses bring (Stone, 1989). As a result, from providing resources for public-private partnerships to shaping policy to holding office, business leaders dominate local politics.

While scholars have focused on the centrality of businesses to American urban politics for the better part of a century (Burns, 2003; Dahl, 1961; Kirkland, 2021; Molotch, 1976), only recently has attention focused on how men dominate these powerful positions and thus local politics (Kirkland, 2022). Because the economy and access to resources are highly gendered in the United States, so is business ownership and power. Although women are half of all workers, the US Census finds that just 12 per cent of businesses are owned by women. And those firms control fewer resources: the average earnings of workers in women-owned businesses lag behind those businesses owned by men (US Census Bureau, 2021). These gender imbalances are especially visible among larger businesses, where women are just 6 per cent of Fortune 500 CEOs and hold less than 20 per cent of corporate board seats (Lyness & Grotto, 2018).[20] Women-owned businesses pay their employees less.[21] The gender gap in business ownership and power also has implications for the marginalisation of racial and ethnic minorities. Men are nearly two-thirds (65 per cent) of white business owners, while men make up just over half (55 per cent) of Black business owners (Leppert, 2023).

Gender segregation among occupations also extends to women and men who own businesses. Women own a larger share of businesses relating to health care and social assistance, while they are less likely to own firms in sectors like construction and finance (Hait, 2021). Because the types of firms that men own generate more resources, this further exacerbates the firm value differences for men and women. These differences may have implications for both their ability to run for office and their acceptability as candidates to voters. While local elections in California are nominally non-partisan, candidates can certainly espouse progressive or conservative ideologies and choose to fundraise most heavily from unions, businesses, small or large donors, and so on. As M., a consultant at an Emerge training, said, 'Two things get people elected to office: money, and I can't remember what the other thing is.'

---

[20] Efforts to increase women's representation on corporate boards include gender quotas; these quotas then increase attention to gender equity issues by companies (Latura & Weeks, 2022).

[21] Women-owned firms paid their employees an annual wage of $38,238 compared with $54,114 for firms owned by men in 2019 (Hait, 2021).

Women's exclusion from the primary business pipeline to office is also indicative of women's lack of access to broader networks of power in their local communities (Cruz, Labonne, & Querubín, 2017; S. C. McGregor & Mourão, 2016). Homophily in networks (where 'like works with like') contributes to women's exclusion from powerful positions (McPherson, Smith-Lovin, & Cook, 2001). Men and white people in power recruit new candidates from their social networks (Crowder-Meyer, 2013; Ocampo, 2018; Sweet-Cushman, 2020b); those networks happen to largely be made up of other men, especially white men, and especially white men with their same or similar professional backgrounds. This then produces what Crowder-Meyer (2013) calls 'gendered recruitment without trying'. Elite networks' power in local politics is visible through how interest groups, political organisations, and political parties recruit and support candidates for office (Anzia, 2022; Benjamin & Miller, 2019). Even in an environment like California where local elections are entirely non-partisan, local political parties are still powerful forces for candidate emergence and success (Burnett, 2019; Heerde & Bowler, 2007).

How does the dominance of 'it's not what you know, it's who you know' in local politics influence the gender balance of candidates and winners? How does it shape the occupation and gender of candidates? Far less attention has focused on how local networks and parties might help or hinder women seeking office, or how these networks might vary by the occupation of individuals. As Tolley and Paquet (2021, p. 41) note, 'party organization and strategy should be given greater attention in the literature on women's representation, particularly at the municipal level'. Indeed, in one of the Emerge trainings on fundraising, women were told to 'be careful about calling folks like developers, who may be controversial' (J., Consultant). The implications of such advice may be that women are less well connected to the local business community, less well-resourced, and less likely to win their elections.[22]

In other words, if:

1. businesses are intertwined with local politics because they provide necessary economic resources for cities, *and*
2. women are less likely to be in business, and when in business, to have access to the same kinds of resources and networks than men in business have, *then*
3. local leadership will include fewer women than men, even if women and men with business backgrounds win office at similar rates.

---

[22] Such advice may be party-specific.

Teachers Can Be Powerful, But Seek Few Local Offices

When Americans are asked about the honest and ethical standards of people from different professions, grade school teachers have the third highest rating (after nurses and doctors) (Gallup, 2022). Almost two-thirds of the American public (64 per cent) rate the group as having very high or high standards. In comparison, Americans rate lawyers (19 per cent rated very high or high), local office holders (22 per cent), and business executives (15 per cent) at much lower rates than teachers. Not only that: teachers and educators are generally middle-class, educated, and deeply invested in the outcomes of local political debates. And, teachers, teachers' unions, and education policy are at the centre of local political debates across the country (Lay, 2022; Lay & Tyburski, 2017).

A background in education also provides many of the same networking and organisational resources that those in the business community enjoy (Hartney, 2023). Women have a long history of involvement in teaching and healthcare unions; indeed, Emerge California devoted a whole section of a training day to 'Women and Organized Labor'. A recent evaluation of the role that unions play in training teachers as candidates for political office finds that unions act as 'schools of democracy', cultivating political engagement and ambition and supporting candidates when they run (Lyon, Hemphill, & Jacobsen, 2022). Teachers' unions can be especially powerful in local politics, too: as S., a former state party leader, said to a roomful of potential political candidates, 'whatever the labor people say, just listen.' (Had we observed a training with conservative women, they might well be giving the opposite advice.) This party leader is not wrong: as Hartney (2023) finds, 'teachers' unions remain an influential player in local school politics today.' This is true not just in the United States, but around the world (Chambers-Ju, 2014; Moe & Wiborg, 2016).

And yet—perhaps because teachers are overwhelmingly women—the role of educators in local politics has received far less attention than the role of business leaders by scholars of urban politics. Similarly, work on political ambition and women in political office has largely ignored educators as a potential pool for recruitment, although work by scholars like Deckman (2004) and Sweet-Cushman (2020b) offer a much-needed examination of school board candidates, who often have backgrounds in education and are women (see Figure 10). This work finds that women from education backgrounds are much more likely to run for school board than other local offices, but are less likely to run for higher office. This is also true in other countries; for example, Davidson, McGregor, and Siemiatycky (2020, p. 461) study school board elections in Canada and find that 'while women do very well in school board elections,

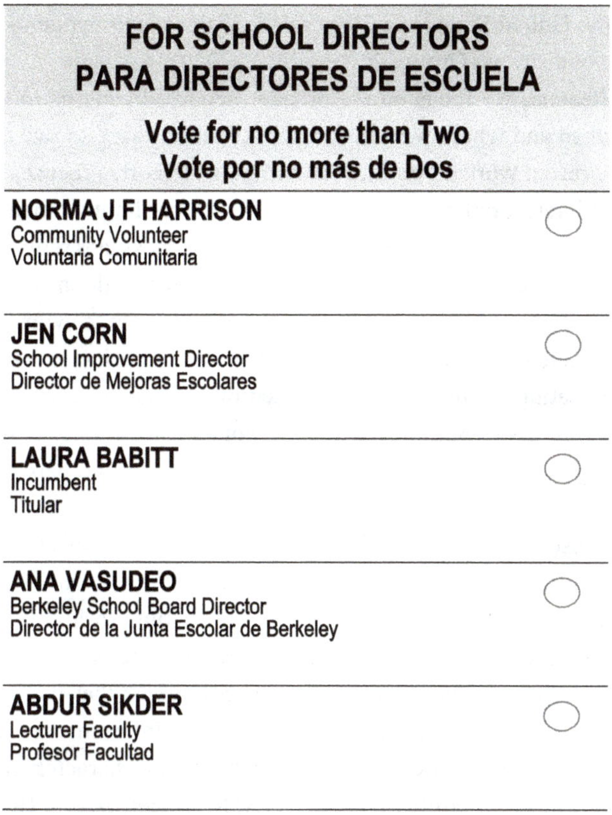

FOR SCHOOL DIRECTORS
PARA DIRECTORES DE ESCUELA

Vote for no more than Two
Vote por no más de Dos

NORMA J F HARRISON
Community Volunteer
Voluntaria Comunitaria

JEN CORN
School Improvement Director
Director de Mejoras Escolares

LAURA BABITT
Incumbent
Titular

ANA VASUDEO
Berkeley School Board Director
Director de la Junta Escolar de Berkeley

ABDUR SIKDER
Lecturer Faculty
Profesor Facultad

Figure 10 Education on the ballot. Sample ballot from Santa Barbara County, CA.

they are significantly less likely than their male counterparts to have the desire to move up to provincial or federal politics'.

5.1 Voter Demand for Business Leaders and Educators

Women's advantage from holding positions in education, particularly as teachers of earlier years of education, does not necessarily extend to women seeking leadership positions within education (Lee & Mao, 2023). The share of women who are principals and vice principals has more than doubled in the past thirty years. Even so, women advance more slowly on administrative career paths than men do in education (Bailes & Guthery, 2020).[23] Such differences extend to superintendents; for example, women are 24 per cent of superintendents

[23] For example, Bailes and Guthery (2020, p. 1) find that even though women are more qualified when they become assistant principals, 'they are less likely to be promoted to high school principal, and when they are, it is after a longer assistant principalship'.

overall in the United States and 29 per cent of the superintendents of the 500 largest school districts (Group, 2023; NSBA, 2020).[24]

In this Element, we focus on the broader gendered patterns in society that constrain when and where women run for office. In doing so, we depart from much of the recent work on political ambition, which often focuses on individual levels of interest rather than structural factors that limit women's access to power (e.g., Fox & Oxley, 2003). We also see these messages replicated among those seeking to increase women's representation in educational leadership. For example, the National School Board Association points to women's interest as a key obstacle to increasing the share of women as principals and superintendents: 'Creating the best pipeline for senior leadership means encouraging women to apply' (NSBA, 2020). Our work points to the futility of relying only on increasing individual interest as a tool for resolving the gaps in women's officeholding.

But it is also possible that this is not entirely a story of supply but also demand. That is, voters may be exposed to fewer women with business backgrounds and more women teachers on the ballot, thus shrinking the pool of women with masculine backgrounds and increasing the pool of women from feminine backgrounds. Voters may also simply *prefer* that the women they select for positions have feminine backgrounds. Unfortunately for women, voters *also prefer* that political leaders have masculine characteristics, particularly for some kinds of political positions (N. M. Bauer, 2020a; Holman et al., 2022; Oliver & Conroy, 2018).[25] That is, voters generally believe that holding some political offices is a masculine activity and want leaders who have the experiences or characteristics that fit with the masculinity of the office.

The 'think leader-think man' pattern of decision-making also extends to other forms of leadership beyond politics. A broad set of scholarship finds that when people think about business success and managerial prowess, they think about men (Schein & Davidson, 1993; Sczesny, 2003). As a result, people regularly discount women's experience as 'not managerial', and women's advancement up the ladder in corporate jobs around the world is made more difficult by these stereotypes (Y. Kim & Weseley, 2017). Gender stereotypes of teachers also reveal that parents, other teachers, and administrators all want teachers with communal skills (Anliak & Beyazkurk, 2008). Because people associate women with communal skills (and often perceive men in education, particularly earlier years of teaching, as 'weird' or

---

[24] This extends to California, where women run 28 per cent of large school districts.
[25] But see Bernhard (2022) for exceptions.

homosexual; see S. B. Murray, 1996; Sumsion, 2000), women are privileged in seeking positions in education.

When we examine the individual positions associated with business in the CEDA data, we see quite a bit of diversity in specific occupations that candidates list. Within our group of candidates, the broad category of 'chief executives' makes up more than 60 per cent of the candidates; within that category, we have business owners (20 per cent of all those in the business category) and executives (just under 5 per cent).[26] Managers (11 per cent) and business operations jobs (16 per cent) are also common.

Educators also list a variety of occupations on the ballot, although the category is dominated by teachers, who make up more than 50 per cent of the candidates in the education category. These include a diversity of specific positions, including occupations like 'elementary school teachers' or 'science teachers'. People working at universities and in school administration are also common: professors and university faculty make up 14 per cent of the candidates, and school administrators like principals are 6 per cent of the candidates.

When we examine gender distributions across business leaders and educators and within these broader categories, three patterns stand out. First, women are underrepresented among business leaders (making up 28 per cent of candidates with this background) *and* educators (making up 40 per cent of candidates). Second, among business leaders, there are almost no gender differences *within* the subcategories; for example, six of ten women and six in ten men with a business background are business owners or executives. And, third, among educators, women are more likely to list teaching as their job (55 per cent of women vs 50 per cent of men) and less likely to list jobs like school administrators (4.5 per cent of women vs 7.6 per cent of men) or university professors (12 per cent of women and 16 per cent of men).

We next examine whether business and education backgrounds help candidates seeking political office, by office and candidate gender. These results are presented in Figure 11. To do so, we estimate models of the likelihood of a candidate winning a particular election if they list a business occupation (top pane) or education-related occupation (bottom pane) against all other occupations. On the y-axis, we list each office; the offices are organised by the relative probability of winning the office, given a business (top pane) or education (bottom pane) background.[27] We provide estimates for both men and

---

[26] There are, of course, variations in these listings, from candidates calling themselves a 'local business owner' to writing that they own a book, record, or media store, for example.

[27] Here, the occupation codings from CEDA ballot designations are non-exclusive, in that candidates can have multiple codings and thus appear more than once. This allows us to count those

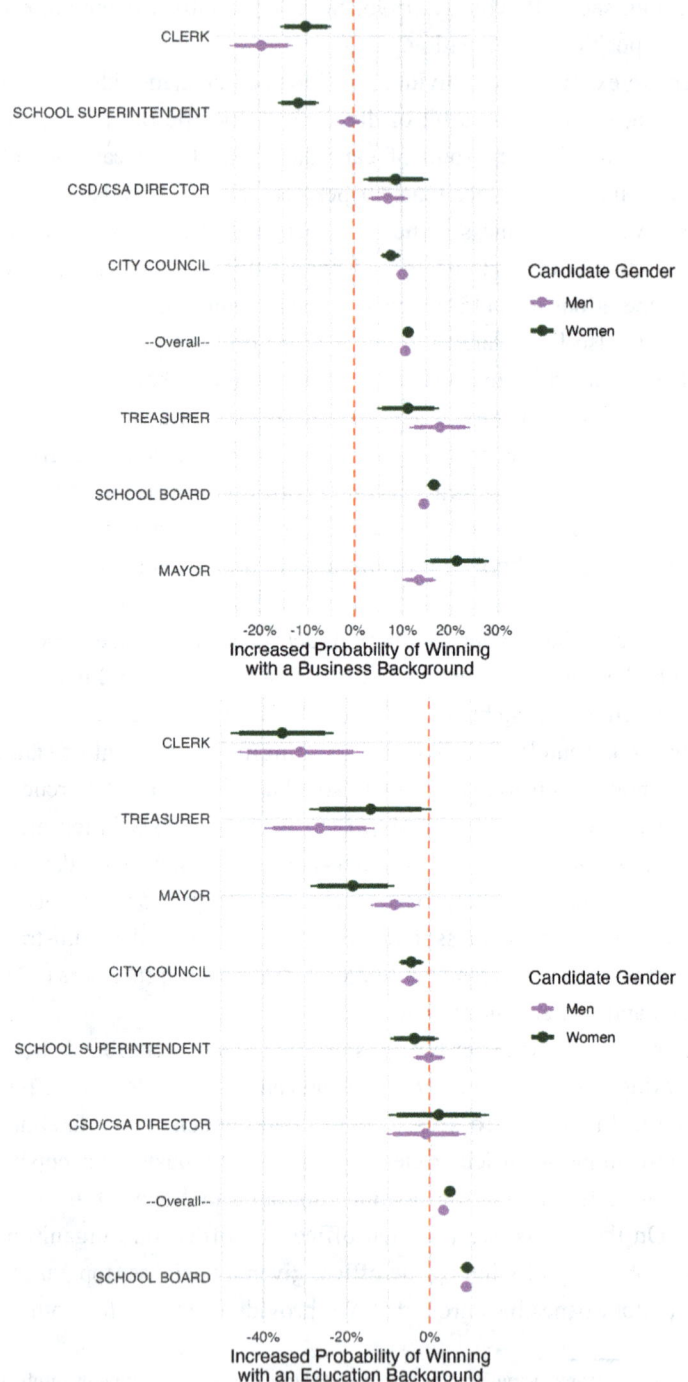

Figure 11 The probability of winning an elected for men and women with business and education backgrounds. CEDA Data.

women with backgrounds in business and education for the overall pool (the 'overall' coefficient) and for each office in our dataset.

As we might expect, a business background is an asset for candidates in most local elections, as we show in the top pane of Figure 11. To start, we can see in the 'overall' category that both men and women with business backgrounds win rates at higher rates than do any other occupational categories. Not only that, but business leaders are more likely to win *every* office except clerk and school superintendent. We see similar rates of winning for men and women, except for school superintendents, where businesswomen are less likely to win and businessmen are equally likely to win, as compared to other occupations.

In comparison, an educational background really only advantages men and women who are seeking school board positions. We see an overall effect, but we can attribute this to the large number of school board elections that we have in the CEDA data. For the 'core' urban politics positions of mayor, councillor, treasurer, and clerk, an education background reduces the likelihood of winning an election as compared to other occupations. And men and women from educational backgrounds have similar fates on the ballot: that is, neither men nor women teachers are more or less able to translate their occupations into electoral victories.

The results presented in Figure 11 show *little* evidence of gender biases by voters once business leaders and teachers are on the ballot: being in a feeder occupation is far more impactful than the combination of gender and occupation. But as we show in Figure 6 and Table 1, the rate by which men and women hold these positions and then emerge as candidates differs considerably. Our work provides more evidence for the importance of considering candidate emergence as one of the primary obstacles to gender equity in political office (e.g. Bernhard et al., 2018; Conroy, 2016; Holman & Schneider, 2018). While these offices are non-partisan, we also know that the ideological and partisan make-up of business owners and teachers differ considerably (Wade, 2018); for example, DeWitt (2021) finds that business leaders are mostly Republicans. One consequence may be that, even for non-partisan local offices, this occupational-partisan sorting results in Republican leaders dominating offices like mayor while Democrats are more common on school boards.

In sum, we've learned that while having particular jobs in business and education translate into a substantial advantage on Election Day, a business background seems to help one advance to nearly any kind of political office,

---

who list occupational combinations like 'businessman/entertainment director' or 'teacher and pastor' on the ballot.

while education offers a substantial but very narrow boost for school board races alone. We also learned that this is likely due at least in part to the different stories underlying their dominance in politics: businesses and business people fund city halls and have dense political connections. On the other hand, while educators are seen as trustworthy and education is powerful (often thanks to its union connections), that power seems to translate to advantages in seeking positions on the school board alone. In the next section, we explore in more detail just why it is that the experiences of those in these occupations varies so much across local offices.

6 Voters See Some Local Offices as Feminine and Less Prestigious

The gender role socialisation patterns that we have focused on throughout this Element have implications for women running for office, including the types and levels of office (Crowder-Meyer & Lauderdale, 2014; Sweet-Cushman, 2021). Generally, women leaders expect to receive (and do receive) biased assessments because the communal characteristics that society ascribes to women do not meet the agentic expectations that society has for leadership roles (N. M. Bauer & Santia, 2023; Bernhard et al., 2021; Holman, Mahoney, & Hurler, 2021). However, these expectations about leadership roles are not static across offices. Executive offices, including mayors and county executives, and those associated with masculine issues, like sheriffs and prosecutors, have higher levels of agentic expectations (Bernhard et al., 2021; Farris & Holman, 2023a; Sweet-Cushman, 2021). Legislative offices, including city councils and county commissions, and those associated with feminine issues, like school boards and city clerks, have lower levels of agentic expectations (Anzia & Bernhard, 2022; Crowder-Meyer et al., 2015; Kellogg et al., 2019; McBrayer & Williams, 2022; Sweet-Cushman, 2021) and thus may be friendlier spaces for women's ambition.

The non-partisan nature of local politics in the United States further reduces the ability of voters to evaluate the behaviour of candidates (Trounstine, 2009). In an era of high levels of polarisation, partisanship is one of the most important factors for voters making up their minds (Bernhard & Freeder, 2020; de Benedictis-Kessner & Warshaw, 2016). Without that party label, voters will try to infer candidates' ideologies from other clues (Holman & Lay, 2021) – and gender, race, and even occupation all tend to be easily inferred from names and ballot designations. In effect, voters 'fill in' the information they don't have by relying on these pieces of information, which saves them from having to look up more detailed (but more accurate) information (N. M. Bauer, 2020b; Matson & Fine, 2006; McDermott, 1997, 2005). As we discuss in the introduction, this can lead to a heavy reliance on gender and racial stereotypes.

While a broad body of scholarship has demonstrated the centrality of *gender* stereotypes for voter decision-making (Aaldering & Pas, 2020; Bernhard, 2022; Holman, 2016b; Huddy & Terkildsen, 1993; Lay et al., 2021) and for potential candidates deciding to run for office (Lazarus & Steigerwalt, 2018; Schneider et al., 2016; Sweet-Cushman, 2016), we know less about how *occupation* might interact to exacerbate or remedy these stereotypes. We know that information helps voters make informed decisions (Crowder-Meyer et al., 2019; Kam & Zechmeister, 2013), but that voters will sometimes ignore information that is counter to their existing stereotypes about women in office (N. M. Bauer, 2020a, 2020b; Holman et al., 2017, 2018).

We argue that the use of gender and racial stereotypes in election decisions can be *exacerbated* for offices where the voters know little about the candidates or are unable to assess what a 'good' candidate might look like for a given office. Research on voting for sheriffs and prosecutors, for example, shows that voters rarely make connections between their policy preferences and the vote choice (de Benedictis-Kessner, Einstein, & Palmer, 2023; Farris & Holman, 2024; Sances, 2017, 2021).[28]

We thus expect that voters will use a combination of occupation and gender to assess the capacity of any individual candidate to hold a particular office. Because offices themselves are gendered, the gender and occupation of the office sends powerful signals to voters about which candidates will be capable of carrying out the work of the office. And, because candidates for office are highly strategic (Anzia & Bernhard, 2022; Barnes & Holman, 2020a; Fulton et al., 2006; Kanthak & Woon, 2015; Ondercin, 2022), women will be more likely to run for offices where their gender and occupation give them an advantage in voters' minds.

While previous literature has established that political offices, like jobs, are gender-typed (Anzia & Bernhard, 2022; Crowder-Meyer et al., 2015), we argue that offices are also gender-occupation-typed. If, for instance, the prototypical school board candidate is a teacher, this is likely to produce gendered occupational selection patterns, not simply occupational selection patterns. We then ask how these patterns match (or do not) what voters believe to be

---

[28] This is not just a problem with more 'obscure' offices: even when well-informed voters are selecting mayoral candidates, their vote choices rarely line up with their discrete policy positions (Holman & Lay, 2021).

the most common and most desirable occupations by office. As of yet, the gender-occupation-typology of offices has yet to be fully explored.

Importantly, while our data is on the United States, we expect gender-occupation office typing to exist in other places, although the exact offices and contents of those stereotypes may vary. For instance, in the United Kingdom, police and crime commissioners may have a similar office-occupation typing, and in turn gender-occupation typing (in 2023 approximately 35 per cent of police officers in England and Wales were women, Allen & Carthew, 2024). Schwindt-Bayer (2011) shows that in Argentina, women legislators are more likely to come from an education profession and to serve or have served in city councils. Although positions with very specific portfolios (like Minister of Health or Commissioner on the Status of Women) are appointed, rather than elected, in most countries, there is substantial evidence that these practices are gendered in ways that produce more women in feminine-typed and low-prestige ministries than masculine-typed or high-prestige ministries (Barnes & O'Brien, 2018; Kroeber & Hüffelmann, 2022; Siklodi, Ie, & Allen, 2023). Interestingly, Davis (2007) has shown that in 'specialist systems' of government, where ministers are selected based on their relevant experience and occupation rather than, for example, their party membership, women are better represented than in generalist systems. However, this finding seems to be a function of how few women were serving in parliaments (and thus eligible to be selected in a generalist system) at the time than a function of how selecting on occupation or relevant experience would be expected to benefit women (Claveria, 2014). In short, while we do not provide evidence here that there are similar gender-occupation office typing effects around the world, there is nothing about gender, occupation, or office role congruity that suggests local offices in the United States are the only place our theory would apply.

6.1 Local Offices Vary in Femininity and Prestige

In this section, we first show that *offices* are typed as masculine or feminine by voters and that this corresponds with the share of women who hold those offices. In comparison to previous work on local offices that shows the application of gender stereotypes by inferring voter stereotypes (Anzia & Bernhard, 2022; Crowder-Meyer et al., 2015) or survey and experimental data that asks about generic offices, a single local office, or about comparisons across national-level legislative and executive offices (N. M. Bauer, 2018; I. Cargile, 2015; Oliver & Conroy, 2018; Schneider & Bos, 2014; Sweet-Cushman, 2021), we explicitly test how voters perceive of the femininity and masculinity of each kind of local office. To do so, we rely again on the LUCID survey data we described in Section 2.

To understand how voters see each office, we drew on the measurement strategy created by Bittner and Goodyear-Grant (2017) and asked people to rate each office on a femininity to masculinity scale. The rating extends from '0–100, where 0 represents offices that are 100% masculine and 100 represents offices that are 100% feminine' but instead of occupations as we did before, we asked about offices: 'Some political offices are seen as more feminine, while others are seen as more masculine.' The responses to this produce, for each office, a measure of *office femininity*. We also asked the respondents to rate each office on the same prestige scale as we asked about occupations, borrowed from the General Social Survey: 'Where would you place each political office in terms of its social standing?' Respondents placed offices on a scale from 1 ('if you think it has the lowest possible social standing') to 9 ('the highest possible social standing'). We use this as a measure of *office prestige*. For both ratings, we asked about 13 common local offices in the CEDA data, with each person in the survey rating ten occupations, randomly assigned: City Council, City Clerk, Community Services Director, District Attorney, Judge, Mayor, Police Chief, Rent Control Board Member, School Board Member, School Superintendent, Sheriff, and Treasurer.

We ask about a wide share of local offices because these are offices where voters must select a relevant candidate on a regular basis. As Sumner et al. (2020) note, 'Every day is election day in America', and the set of offices that Americans vote on includes the mundane and the obscure. For example, while voters around the world are generally familiar with the office of a mayor, many other offices are either uniquely American (like a sheriff) or vary in their appearance on a ballot across states or even across cities. For example, in California, many cities have created institutional bodies to engage in advocacy, advising, policymaking, and adjudication over rent and rent control in the city. Some cities (such as San Francisco, which has the highest rental rate in the nation) created an appointed board where members are appointed by the mayor to balance landlord and tenant representation. Other cities created elected positions. For instance, Santa Monica's rent control board is fully elected, and in 2022, the three candidates who won 'listed their careers [on the ballot as follows]: Ivanov an attorney, Lesley a healthcare worker and Gonska in entertainment marketing' (Sawicki, 2022).

Understanding the characteristics of candidates and elected officials for a wide set of local offices offers both a practical advancement over the existing scholarship and an opportunity for new theoretical tests. Scholars have long pointed to local offices as perhaps the most likely place to see gender stereotypes; after all, voters are neither interested in seeking out information about candidates (Cruz, Keefer, & Labonne, 2021; R. M. McGregor et al., 2017;

Nordin, 2014) nor are they equipped to know how to seek out information (Bernhard & Freeder, 2020; Holman & Lay, 2021). Institutional features like election timing and ballot design – many of which are purposefully designed to suppress turnout and accountability – further limit the ability of voters to obtain accurate and complete information about candidates (Anzia, 2013; de Benedictis-Kessner, 2017; Trounstine, 2010).

We indeed find that people's perceptions of the masculinity and femininity of offices a) vary considerably and b) correspond with the share of women in those offices.[29] Ratings of femininity range from 34 (for sheriffs) to 65 (for clerks); these perceptions are highly correlated (0.71) with the share of women who actually hold these offices; for example, 5.6 per cent of sheriffs and 62.3 per cent of clerks are women. Consistent with other work that has examined specific offices (Anzia & Bernhard, 2022; Crowder-Meyer et al., 2015, i.e.,) as well as comparative work that finds that ministries and cabinet appointments are similarly gendered (e.g., Armstrong et al., 2022; Kroeber & Hüffelmann, 2022), we take this as evidence that offices themselves are gender-typed, which should influence how powerful people view each office and the degree to which people think that specific jobs are appropriate for the office. A full set of the assessments of femininity and prestige for each office are available in Appendix Table A.1.

6.2 Offices Are 'Occupation Typed', with Gendered Consequences

This first set of data tells us about how voters see particular offices as more masculine or feminine. But recall that we are not just interested in how offices are *gender-typed*, but also how they are *gender-occupation-typed*. To test this, we asked the same set of respondents for a second evaluation:

- Which of the following do you think voters are **more likely** to elect to the office of [office]?

where the office is a randomised selection of one of the offices that were evaluated on the masculine-feminine and prestige scales. Each respondent is provided two occupations, each of which was chosen from three sets of occupations. We use a question about generic voters following in the footsteps of previous scholars who argue that asking about other voters is a useful means of avoiding social desirability biases (DeMora et al., 2022).[30]

---

[29] This is consistent with work by Stauffer (2021), who finds that voters typically overestimate the share of women in office.
[30] We also asked about personal vote choice in a pre-test and found similar results across the two questions.

These sets of occupations include (1) the most common 'feeder' occupations into local office (legislative aide, incumbent, project manager, CEO, lawyer, business owner); (2) a set of masculine-feminine occupations paired on occupational prestige and class (non-profit director vs accountant, nurse vs doctor, realtor vs real estate developer, teacher vs police officer); and (3) final set of common occupations selected to vary on masculinity-femininity, prestige, and training requirements, including executive assistant, artist, cafeteria worker, college professor, construction worker, architect, military veteran, rancher, banker, teacher's aide, librarian, and pizza deliveryman. Randomisation processes mean that each respondent evaluated 15 occupational pairs across two offices.

We start our analysis of this data by asking: do voters see those jobs as most common feeder careers as best suited for a particular office? We examine this by looking at the most common occupations for each job in the observational data and the degree to which voters selected those same occupations as the better fit and more likely to be elected; the full list of comparisons we directly make is in Appendix Table A.2.

Next, we examine the degree to which voters want offices filled with individuals who are by profession qualified to hold the office, 'linking professional experience to the office in question' (Atkeson & Hamel, 2020, p. 60). In this case, we would see strong correspondence between the occupation's portfolio and the office's portfolio. To do so, we look at three offices and sets of occupations: school board or school superintendent and teachers, college professors, teacher's aides, and librarians; sheriff and police chief and police officer and military veterans; and city clerk and administrative assistant and legislative aide.

Survey respondents were asked to choose between two jobs for a given office. In Figure 12, the y-axis represents how often they picked a given job over the other job presented, and the x-axis represents the perceived femininity of a given job; the offices are ordered from most masculine (sheriff, upper left) to most feminine (school board member, bottom right). The dotted line shows the overall direction of the relationship between these two variables. When the line slopes down from left to right (a negative slope), respondents thought individuals with more feminine jobs were less electable to that office. When the line slopes up (a positive slope), more feminine jobs are seen as more electable for a given office.

Generally, people see jobs that correspond to the work of a position as most appropriate for that position. In Figure 12, we have organised similar types of jobs together; on the y-axis, we have the perceived electability. Each dot represents an individual occupation from our survey data. In the top row, we

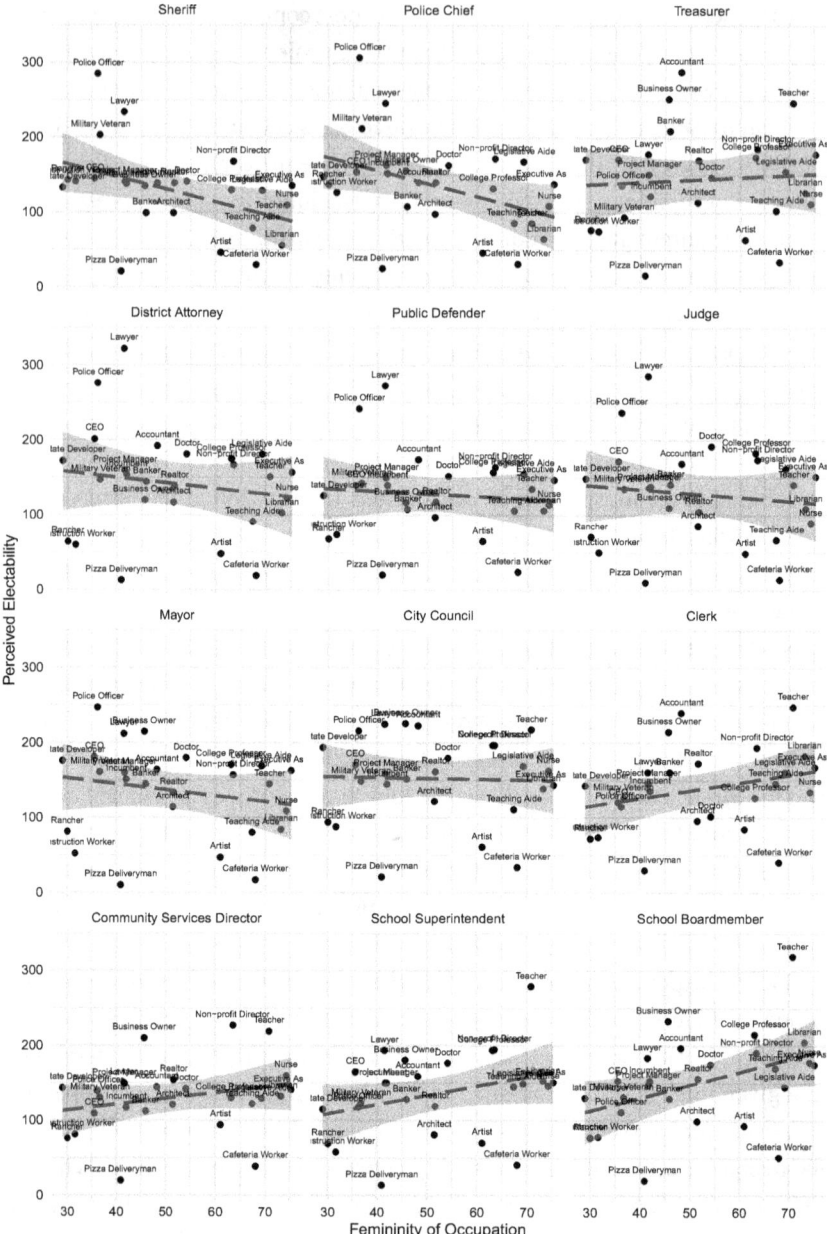

Figure 12 More feminine occupations are more electable for more feminine offices, and less electable to masculine offices. Original survey data.

can see that police, lawyers, and military veterans are all seen as best for the jobs of sheriffs and police chiefs. Similarly, accountants are most electable for the office of treasurer. And teachers are seen as most electable for both school board and school superintendent positions. But we also see the discounting of lower status jobs within and across occupations. Like Atkeson and Hamel (2020), we find that people see teachers as most electable, but not teacher's aides. And even though the work of a clerk is much akin to that of an administrative assistant, that job is not seen as electable as a business owner or accountant. And low-status jobs like pizza delivery man and cafeteria worker are seen as least electable across all offices.[31]

But it is not just specific jobs that are important: we can see in Figure 12 that respondents match the femininity of the office with the electability of specific occupations. Candidates running for offices with 'masculine' portfolios, like sheriff and police chief, are more electable when they hold more masculine jobs. Similarly, offices with 'feminine' portfolios, like school board and community services director, seemed most achievable for candidates holding more feminine jobs. Some offices, like city council, fell somewhere in the middle: respondents felt that candidates could be equally successful with either feminine or masculine jobs.

We depict this data a little more simply in Figure 13. Here, we can see that the offices where respondents perceive having a feminine job as key to electability are much more likely to be offices with feminine portfolios, like school board, and the reverse holds for masculine jobs and offices with masculine portfolios. Many of these differences are not statistically significant, but if we were to fit a regression between the femininity of the office and the perceived likelihood of being elected out of a feminine job, we would see a strong relationship.

Next, we look at how this translates into real election data. Figure 14 shows how likely candidates are to win their elections as a function of the ratings of femininity of their jobs (as listed in their ballot designation). Let's break down this chart. For each unit that a job becomes more feminine (recall that our scale is 0–100, where 0 represents exclusively masculine jobs and 100 exclusively feminine jobs), a candidate running for sheriff is about 2.5 percentage points less likely to win their race.

We can also understand this in terms of the average differences in ratings across occupations, as measured by the standard deviation. One standard deviation on the feminine occupation scale is about 11.1 points: roughly, the difference between mining machine operators (the most masculine-rated occupation in our data, at 19.5) and industrial truck and tractor operators (rated at 30.8), or between nurse midwives (at 83.0, the most feminine-rate

---

[31] We take this positive sign of the validity of the exercise – respondents were paying attention and saw these jobs as lower in status.

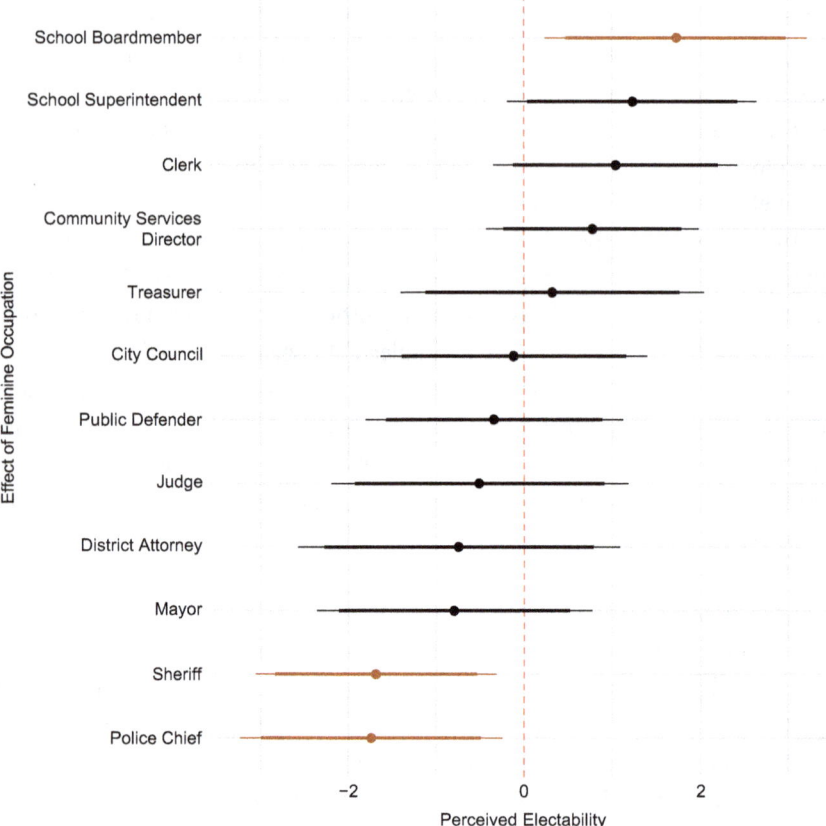

Figure 13 More feminine jobs are better fit for more feminine offices, and worse fits for masculine offices; survey data. Original survey data.

occupation in our data) and medical records and health information technicians (at 72.3). So, if a nurse midwife runs for sheriff, she would be about 25 percentage points less likely to win her race than a medical records technician. Of course, these estimates don't translate well in many cases: there are no nurse midwives running for sheriff in our data, for instance, so we should be cautious about predicting real elections from these estimates.

Recall that in Section 4, we found that the more feminine the occupation, the better a candidate's odds of winning an election were. Here, we show that the story is more nuanced: feminine occupations do help significantly across many offices, but for some very masculine-typed offices, including mayoral races, feminine occupations hurt rather than help candidates.

Broadly, then, we see a close correspondence between the survey and the election data: candidates with masculine jobs running for masculine offices

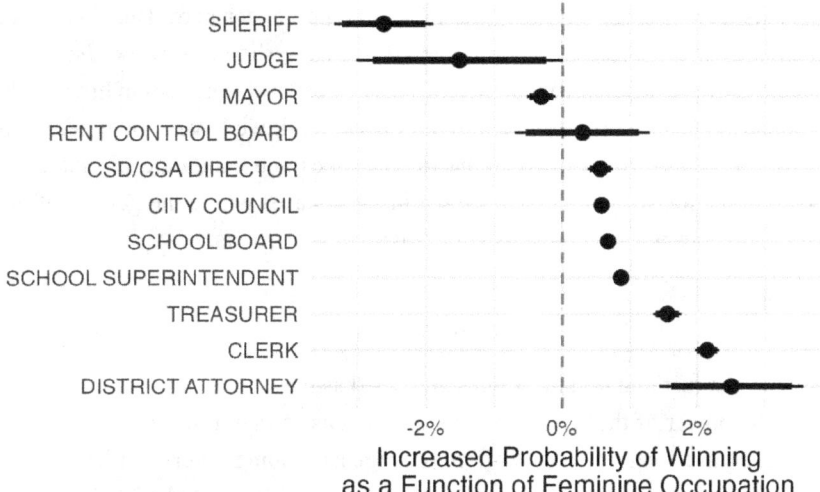

Figure 14 More feminine jobs seem to help candidates win some types of races, and hurt in others. CEDA data: Feminine jobs seem to help candidates most in feminine offices like clerk, and hurt candidates running for masculine offices like sheriff. Estimates derived from regressions that include fixed effects for county and year, and are depicted with 90 per cent confidence intervals (thick bars) and 95 per cent confidence intervals (thin bars).

tended to fare better in both survey and election data, and the same was true for feminine jobs and feminine offices.[32] It could also be because survey respondents were somewhat unsure about the portfolio of the office (note that, for instance, some respondents may have thought that public defenders were peacekeepers, rating police officers and military veterans highly, rather than lawyers assigned to represent defendants who could not afford counsel). Some of these jobs are also interesting because of rules about required occupational training to hold the job; for example, district attorneys and public defenders in California must be lawyers to hold the position.

Finally, we do not see major differences in the 'effect' of holding a feminine occupation for a given office by the gender of the candidates. While women are advantaged compared to men in more feminine occupations, in most cases these differences are only small fractions of a percentage point.[33]

---

[32] This could be because there are relatively few observations of these elections (e.g., district attorney only has a few hundred observations). It may also be because district attorneys and sheriffs in California are reelected at extraordinarily high rates.

[33] One reason these are statistically significant differences is the large number of elections in our data, for example, for school board.

We thus do not break out our data by candidate gender here. But this is not to say that these offices are not gendered: we have shown in work elsewhere (Anzia & Bernhard, 2022) that there are large gender differences in how likely candidates are to win races for a given office. And, we have shown here that there is a gender role congruity between offices and candidate occupations, such that gender is 'in the room' even in those cases where the gender of the candidate does not make a substantial difference to voters.

6.3 People See Feminine Offices as Less Prestigious

Yet it is not just that certain offices are typed as masculine or feminine; voters view the power of those offices through the lens of masculinity or femininity. Scholars have long pointed to office prestige as shaping voters' willingness to support women for particular positions (Crowder-Meyer et al., 2015; Meeks, 2012; Sweet-Cushman, 2021), but generally have compared legislative to executive or local to state. Here, we can compare specific offices to each other and to evaluations of the prestige of those offices.

Office femininity and the share of women holding the office are highly correlated with perceptions of the power of the office, with more feminine offices seen as less powerful. We present the average femininity rating of each of these offices in Figure 15, accompanied by the perceived prestige of the position (dashed purple line, left axis) share of women as candidates (solid black line, right axis). As the figure shows, perceptions of prestige are highly correlated with both perceptions of femininity of the office and the share of women as candidates for the office. For example, city clerks, of which more than 75 per cent of candidates are women, are seen as highly feminine and have the lowest prestige rating of any of the offices. In comparison, an office like the sheriff, where more than 90 per cent of the candidates are men, is seen as highly masculine and in the top quartile of prestige.

In this section, we focused on how specific offices – not just specific occupations – are gender- and prestige-typed and this influences the occupations that people view as appropriate for those positions. A consequence of this is that feminine-typed occupations are *more* electable for many local offices, which are also seen as feminine (Anzia & Bernhard, 2022; N. M. Bauer, 2018). But at the same time, these are the offices that people see as less prestigious, which may have downstream consequences for which local leaders are then able to run for other offices. Further work might explore how these evaluations work if voters consider occupations on the ballot for state and federal offices.

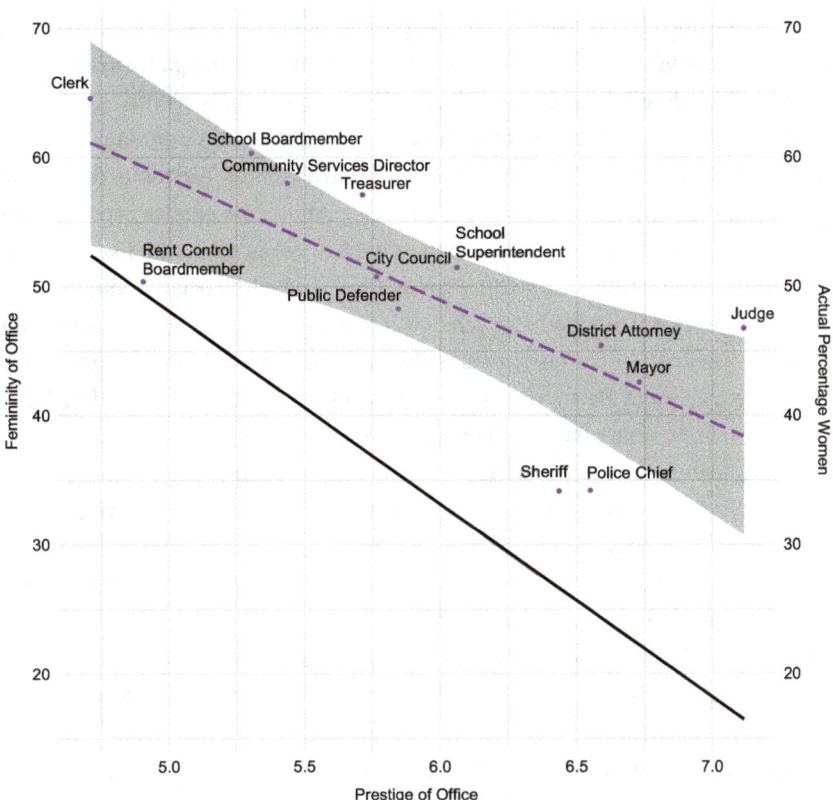

Figure 15 More feminine offices are seen as less prestigious, and fewer women hold more prestigious offices. Purple dashed line: Survey data shows that offices considered more feminine are also evaluated as less prestigious. Solid black line: CEDA data shows that the actual number of women holding office decreases as offices become more prestigious.

7 Work Is Gendered, Politics Is Gendered, and Ambition Is Gendered

> I have a responsibility to push the boundaries of what is considered acceptable for women.
>
> – *D., Board of Education Trustee*

Scholars have long pointed to the fact that gender structures all parts of modern society. Our work draws together two central ways that gender structures our lives: work and politics. In this text, we have focused on the exclusion of women from political office via occupational pathways to candidacy and election. Using a full census of the occupations of candidates for local office in California, survey, and experimental data, we show that the pathways to local office are gendered, with consequences for who runs and wins office.

We use the complete universe of data from candidates running for local office—but only for a single state in the United States. We focus deeply on gender—to the exclusion of race and ethnicity. And while gender gaps in occupation are found across race and ethnic groups, there is substantial variation in the forms of labour across those groups as well. And while occupation, income, and class are bundled together, each does not completely replace the other. Our focus on occupation is thus a weak substitute for deeper investigations of the way that money and class structure access to politics (Elsässer & Schäfer, 2022, 2023). We hope future work will engage more deeply with these questions. For example, we see both police officers and teachers on the ballot—two jobs with similar classes and occupations; research might consider how voters evaluate these types of gender-coded occupations in an experimental context.

Similarly, although our work is consistent with much of what has been found about the gendered appointments of ministers in other countries (Kroeber & Hüffelmann, 2022), it is unclear whether this is due solely to decisions to place women in lower-prestige and stereotype-consistent ministries, or whether the occupational backgrounds of the men and women being appointed also plays a role in maintaining this sort of political gender segregation.

We also do not engage fully with how part-time and home labour shapes women's ability to engage in politics: stay-at-home moms may have more time for seeking political office (maybe!), but may lack access to networks of power and the financial resources needed to successfully seek office. While voters rate women with children more positively than childless women (Stalsburg, 2010; Sweet-Cushman & Bauer, 2024), the formidable structural barriers that keep stay-at-home parents off the ballot remain unexplored.

So much of what we know about voters focuses on presidential or congressional elections, but voters regularly make a wide set of decisions about offices beyond these national positions. Indeed, voters are asked much more frequently to decide local positions than to vote on the president (de Benedictis-Kessner, Lee, et al., 2023). How do voters evaluate the importance of different offices? Our work on the femininity of offices and office prestige is, to our knowledge, a novel way of examining how voters compare candidates and offices to one another, though related to work that classifies ministries by prestige and femininity (see, e.g., Siklodi et al., 2023). But here again, we focus exclusively on local offices and offices that are on the ballot in California. Future work might include an examination of how voters evaluate local, state, and national offices in terms of prestige. This work might help us understand whether the decision-making structures that guide voters to choose a presidential or congressional candidate are the same or different as those used to select a sheriff or a city council member or a rent control board member.

Our focus has also been exclusively on descriptive representation: that is, what shapes whether women, people from specific occupational backgrounds, and women from those occupational backgrounds run for and are elected. At the core of our argument is that descriptive representation matters: a democracy that systematically excludes large segments of its population, particularly groups who have been traditionally marginalised, is not a healthy democracy (Mansbridge, 2015). Indeed, we may not be able to call it a democracy at all (R. Murray, 2014; Paxton, 2000). Thus, understanding when and how we continue to face deep imbalances in who holds office is key to unlocking a better and more democratic system for all.

Yet descriptive representation is also important because it signals to the public that the system is fair, inspiring more trust in the outcomes even if the outcomes do not change overnight (Clayton, O'Brien, & Piscopo, 2019). As Hannah Pitkin (1967, p. 209) famously notes, representation means 'acting in the interest of the represented, in a manner responsive to them'. We hope this work is also a call to academics interested in broader questions of representation and policymaking. Even as electing a mayor with a business background might not dramatically shift local spending (Kirkland, 2020), business mayors do spend less on housing and development (Kirkland, 2021). Work by Barnes et al. (2021) shows that the representation of specific groups of gendered workers can influence spending by state governments. Future work might consider the ways that gender and occupation intersect to influence how local governments make policy, particularly on issues where people have on-the-ground experience.

And, indeed, the descriptive representation of women in political office does mean changes in the policy process, issues discussed, and policy outcomes (Barnes, 2016; Barnes & Holman, 2023; Holman & Mahoney, 2018; Osborn, 2012). At the local level, women's representation changes the voices heard in the policy process, discussions of policy issues, the characteristics of bureaucrats, and policy outcomes (Anzia & Berry, 2011; Funk, 2015; Funk & Molina, 2021; Funk & Philips, 2019; Holman, 2015, 2016b; McBrayer & Williams, 2022; Volden Volden, Wiseman, & Wittmer, 2013).

Similarly, the occupations of elected officials matter not just because they shape who runs for and holds office, but also because occupations inform the work that individuals do once in office (Barnes et al., 2023; Elsässer & Schäfer, 2022; O'Grady, 2019). After his election to the Rent Control Board in Santa Monica, Daniel Ivanov, a lawyer, spoke directly to why his occupation might matter: 'My diverse legal background will allow me to examine disputes between tenants and landlords in a thorough and impartial manner while making sure that the law is applied fairly.' But Ivanov is not just a lawyer; he is also a renter living in a rent-controlled unit. Ivanov argues that these characteristics also matter: 'I live and experience the same issues many of my constituents face which will empower me to serve as their advocate' (Sawicki, 2022).

Future research might consider the ways that gender and occupation interact to shape local political processes and outcomes. Barnes et al. (2023) show, for example, that people trust their national governments more as the representation of the working class increases. Does this apply to local offices, where many people know very little about the functioning of their governments or the names and characteristics of their representatives (Bernhard & Freeder, 2020; de Benedictis-Kessner, 2018)?

Issues also vary in salience across time; these contextual factors may make it easier or harder for members of a particular occupational group to win elections. For example, economic crises may make it more likely that voters select candidates with business backgrounds, while the COVID-19 pandemic might increase interest in medical professionals serving in office (Kirkland, 2021; Lake, 2020). National and state rhetoric or policy around a particular group might also matter: in recent years, teachers have responded to state budget cuts for education by running for office at higher rates (Martinez, 2023). Understanding how the patterns that we have identified here vary across different contexts is an important question for future research.

It may also be that voters reward candidates with feminine occupations because they see these candidates as outsiders and as less corruptible (Barnes, Beaulieu, & Saxton, 2018; Saxton & Barnes, 2022). Corruption is a central issue in local politics (Agerberg, 2020; Ares & Hernández, 2017; Muñoz, Anduiza, & Gallego, 2016).[34] As we discuss in Section 5, some occupations are seen as more trustworthy, including most of the ones dominated by women. Future research might consider when and how the 'demand' for women from specific occupations shifts if there are local instances of corruption. This may also have specific consequences for Black candidates, who are seen as more corrupt by voters (Crawford, 2024).

How to Change These Patterns

One consistent challenge for those seeking office in the United States—including local office—is that money matters. While recent work argues that

---

[34] Although scholars have spent far less time studying this in the United States than in other countries.

the fundraising gap between men and women has largely shrunk (Burrell, 2014), other work points to the excessive work for women in fundraising. In essence, although men and women raise similar amounts of money, women need to source those funds from a broader set of donors, which results in more work for them (Jenkins, 2006). Others point to the uneven burden of fundraising across partisan and race groups (Crowder-Meyer & Cooperman, 2018; Grumbach, Sahn, & Staszak, 2020; J. Kettler, 2020; J. J. Kettler, 2020; Scott, 2022; Scott Brown, Frasure, & Pinderhughes, 2021; Sorensen & Chen, 2022; Swers & Thomsen, 2020).

Even as our knowledge about gender, race, and fundraising has increased, we continue to know little about local political campaigns. The existing work on gender and campaign fundraising overwhelmingly focuses on Congressional or state legislative races for many of the same reasons that we lack even basic information about who runs for and holds local office: there are no central databases for information on who is giving or receiving funds for local campaigns. The existing work largely focuses on a handful of larger cities or single-city case studies (B. E. Adams, 2007; Ingalls & Arrington, 1991; Krebs & Turner, 2015; Tolley, Besco, & Sevi, 2022; Tolley & Paquet, 2021; Werner & Mayer, 2007). Investigations of the networks that allow lawyers and business leaders show that they allow access to large amounts of campaign funds (Bonica, 2017, 2020; Kirkland, 2021, 2022) and these networks help men in particular (Bonica, 2020). But we generally know very little about how the occupational backgrounds of candidates—which are deeply gendered—shape their access to fundraising networks and success.

For those interested in serving in local office, connections to networks are essential for political success. One path forward for both advocates and researchers is to consider the role that campaign training and professional associations play in shaping women's emergence as candidates for local office (Hartney, 2023; Kreitzer & Osborn, 2019; Scott, 2022; Shames et al., 2020; Thomsen & Swers, 2017). For example, work on when teachers run for school board positions points to the core role that teachers' unions can play in supporting these candidates (Hartney, 2023). And the power of local political action committees in influencing policy reinforces these forms of political organising as important to shaping the financial context of local politics (Anzia, 2022; Benjamin, 2022; Benjamin & Miller, 2019). Other work on campaign training organisations points to the importance of considering the *content* of campaign trainings for shaping access to networks (Schneider & Sweet-Cushman, 2020; Sweet-Cushman, 2023). The work presented here points to the importance of considering who is in the pipeline, where we draw elected leaders from, and the importance of broad patterns of gender segregation in society.

Appendix A

Appendix

A1 Appendix Tables

Table A.1 Correspondence between jobs in our survey experiment and occupational categories from Census and CEDA data

Job description from survey	Job category from US Census, CEDA data
Accountant	Accountants and auditors
Architect	Architects
Artist	Artists and related workers
Banker	Financial managers
Business Owner	Chief executives
CEO	Chief executives
Cafeteria Worker	Dining room and cafeteria attendants
College Professor	Postsecondary teachers
Construction Worker	Construction labourers
Doctor	Physicians and surgeons
Executive Assistant	Secretaries and administrative assistants
Incumbent	Legislators
Lawyer	Lawyers
Legislative Aide	Paralegals and legal assistants
Librarian	Librarians
Military Veteran	Military
Non-profit Director	Social and community service managers
Nurse	Nurse practitioners
Pizza Deliveryman	Driver/sales workers and truck drivers
Police Officer	Police and sheriff's patrol officers
Project Manager	General and operations managers
Rancher	Farmers
Real Estate Developer	Construction managers
Realtor	Real estate brokers and sales agents
Teacher	Secondary school teachers
Teaching Aide	Teacher assistants

Table A.2 Prestige and femininity ratings for each office, along with the share of women in that office

Office	Respondent Count	Office Femininity[a]	Office Prestige[a]	% Women in Office[b]
City Council	1193	50.74	5.77	30.77
Clerk	1195	64.57	4.71	62.28
Community Services Director	1184	57.98	5.44	28.40
District Attorney	1180	45.41	6.59	21.46
Judge	1191	46.74	7.12	28.07
Mayor	1195	42.57	6.73	21.90
Police Chief	1202	34.20	6.55	33.33
Public Defender	1218	48.26	5.85	48.00
Rent Control Board	1174	50.37	4.91	46.81
School Board	1172	60.29	5.31	46.02
School Superintendent	1192	51.44	6.06	27.90
Sheriff	1214	34.15	6.44	5.61
Treasurer	1220	57.08	5.72	42.69

[a] Mean rating derived from LUCID Survey Data.
[b] Percentage calculated using CEDA Data.

References

Aaldering, L., & Pas, D. J. V. D. (2020). Political Leadership in the Media: Gender Bias in Leader Stereotypes during Campaign and Routine Times. *British Journal of Political Science*, *50*(3), 911–931.

Aalen, L., Kotsadam, A., Pieters, J., & Villanger, E. (2018). Jobs and Political Participation: Evidence from a Field Experiment in Ethiopia. *The Journal of Politics*, *86*(2), 655–671. https://doi.org/10.1017/S0007123417000795.

Adams, B. E. (2007, February). Fundraising Coalitions in Open Seat Mayoral Elections. *Journal of Urban Affairs*, *29*(5), 481–499. Retrieved 13-08-2018, from https://doi.org/10.1111/j.1467-9906.2007.00361.x.

Adams, J., Bracken, D., Gidron, N., et al. (2023). Can't We All Just Get Along? How Women MPs Can Ameliorate Affective Polarization in Western Publics. *American Political Science Review*, *117*(1), 318–324. https://doi.org/10.1017/S0003055422000491.

Agerberg, M. (2020). The Lesser Evil? Corruption Voting and the Importance of Clean Alternatives. *Comparative Political Studies*, *53*(2), 253–287. https://doi.org/10.1177/0010414019852697.

Alesina, A., Stantcheva, S., & Teso, E. (2018). Intergenerational Mobility and Preferences for Redistribution. *American Economic Review*, *108*(2), 521–554. https://doi.org/10.1257/aer.20162015.

Allen, G., & Carthew, H. (2024). *Police Service Strength* (Tech. Rep.). London: UK Parliament.

Anker, R. (1997). Theories of Occupational Segregation by Sex: An Overview. *International Labor Review*, *136*, 315.

Anliak, S., & Beyazkurk, D. S. (2008, October). Career Perspectives of Male Students in Early Childhood Education. *Educational Studies*, *34*(4), 309–317. https://doi.org/10.1080/03055690802034518.

Anzia, S. F. (2013). *Timing and Turnout: How Off-Cycle Elections Favor Organized Groups*. Chicago: University of Chicago Press.

Anzia, S. F. (2022). *Local Interests: Politics, Policy, and Interest Groups in US City Governments*. Chicago: University of Chicago Press.

Anzia, S. F., & Bernhard, R. (2022). Gender Stereotyping and the Electoral Success of Women Candidates: New Evidence from Local Elections in the United States. *British Journal of Political Science*, *52*(4), 1544–1563. https://doi.org/10.1017/S0007123421000570.

Anzia, S. F., & Berry, C. R. (2011). The Jackie (and Jill) Robinson Effect: Why Do Congresswomen Outperform Congressman? *American Journal of Political Science*, *55*(3), 478–493. https://doi.org/10.1111/j.1540-5907.2011.00512.x.

Ares, M., & Hernández, E. (2017). The Corrosive Effect of Corruption on Trust in Politicians: Evidence from a Natural Experiment. *Research & Politics*, *4*(2), 8–17. https://doi.org/10.1177/2053168017714185 .

Armstrong, B., Barnes, T. D., O'Brien, D. Z., & Taylor-Robinson, M. M. (2022, April). Corruption, Accountability, and Women's Access to Power. *The Journal of Politics*, *84*(2), 1207–1213. https://doi.org/10.1086/715989.

Atkeson, L. R., & Hamel, B. T. (2020). Fit for the Job: Candidate Qualifications and Vote Choice in Low Information Elections. *Political Behavior*, *42*, 59–82 doi.org/10.1007/s11109-018-9486-0.

Ba, B., Kaplan, J., Knox, D., et al. (2023). *Political Diversity in US Police Agencies* [Working Paper]. Available at https://dcknox.github.io/files/BaEtAl_PoliticalDiversityPoliceAgencies.pdf.

Badas, A., & Stauffer, K. E. (2023). Gender and Ambition among Potential Law Clerks. *Journal of Law and Courts*, *11*(1), 116–140.

Bailes, L. P., & Guthery, S. (2020, April). Held Down and Held Back: Systematically Delayed Principal Promotions by Race and Gender. *AERA Open*, *6*(2), 1–17. https://doi.org/10.1177/2332858420929298.

Baker, C. K., Billhardt, K. A., Warren, J., Rollins, C., & Glass, N. E. (2010, January). Domestic Violence, Housing Instability, and Homelessness: A Review of Housing Policies and Program Practices for Meeting the Needs of Survivors. *Aggression and Violent Behavior*, *15*(6), 430–439. https://doi.org/10.1016/j.avb.2010.07.005.

Banzhaf, H. S., & Walsh, R. P. (2008). Do People Vote with Their Feet? An Empirical Test of Tiebout. *American Economic Review*, *98*(3), 843–863. https://www.jstor.org/stable/29730097.

Barari, S., & Simko, T. (2023, March). LocalView, a Database of Public Meetings for the Study of Local Politics and Policy-Making in the United States. *Scientific Data*, *10*(1), 135. https://doi.org/10.1038/s41597-023-02044-y.

Barber, M., Butler, D. M., & Preece, J. R. (2016). Gender Inequalities in Campaign Finance. *Quarterly Journal of Political Science*, *11*(2), 219–248. doi: 10.1561/100.00015126.

Barnes, T. D. (2016). *Gendering Legislative Behavior: Institutional Constraints and Collaboration in Argentina*. New York: Cambridge University Press.

Barnes, T. D., Beall, V., & Holman, M. R. (2021). Pink Collar Representation and Policy Outcomes in U.S. states. *Legislative Studies Quarterly*, *46*(1), 119–154. https://doi.org/10.1111/lsq.12286.

Barnes, T. D., & Beaulieu, E. (2014, September). Gender Stereotypes and Corruption: How Candidates Affect Perceptions of Election Fraud. *Politics*

& *Gender*, *10*(3), 365–391. Retrieved 17-06-2015, from doi:10.1017/S17 43923X14000221.

Barnes, T. D., Beaulieu, E., & Saxton, G. (2018). Sex and Corruption: How Sexism Shapes Voters' Responses to Scandal. *Politics, Groups and Identities*, *8*(1), 103–121. https://doi.org/10.1080/21565503.2018.1441725.

Barnes, T. D., & Holman, M. R. (2018, November). Taking Diverse Backgrounds into Account in Studies of Political Ambition and Representation. *Politics, Groups, and Identities*, *7*(4), 829–841. https://doi.org/10.1080/21565503.2018.1532916.

Barnes, T. D., & Holman, M. R. (2020a). Essential Work Is Gender Segregated: This Shapes the Gendered Representation of Essential Workers in Political Office. *Social Science Quarterly*. https://doi.org/10.1111/ssqu.12850.

Barnes, T. D., & Holman, M. R. (2020b). Gender Quotas, Women's Representation, and Legislative Diversity. *Journal of Politics*, *82*(4). https://doi.org/10.1086/708336.

Barnes, T. D., & Holman, M. R. (2023). Pink-Collar Communication: Gender, Occupation, and Communication about COVID on Twitter. In M. Thomas, & S. Franceschet (Eds.), *Gender and Representation during COVID*. Toronto, CA: University of Toronto Press.

Barnes, T. D., Kerevel, Y. P., & Saxton, G. W. (2023). *Working Class Inclusion: Evaluations of Democratic Institutions in Latin America*. Cambridge: Cambridge University Press.

Barnes, T. D., & O'Brien, D. Z. (2018). Defending the Realm: The Appointment of Female Defense Ministers Worldwide. *American Journal of Political Science*, *62*(2), 355–368. https://doi.org/10.1111/ajps.12337.

Bauer, G., & Dawuni, J. (2015). *Gender and the Judiciary in Africa: From Obscurity to Parity?* Routledge.

Bauer, N. M. (2015). Emotional, Sensitive, and Unfit for Office? Gender StereoType Activation and Support Female Candidates. *Political Psychology*, *36*(6), 691–708.

Bauer, N. M. (2018, April). Running Local: Gender Stereotyping and Female Candidates in Local Elections. *Urban Affairs Review*, *56*(1), 96–123. https://doi.org/10.1177/1078087418770807.

Bauer, N. M. (2020a). *The Qualifications Gap: Why Women Must Be Better than Men to Win Political Office*. Cambridge: Cambridge University Press.

Bauer, N. M. (2020b, January). Shifting Standards: How Voters Evaluate the Qualifications of Female and Male Candidates. *The Journal of Politics*, *82*(1), 1–12. https://doi.org/10.1086/705817.

Bauer, N. M. (2022, June). Who Covers the Qualifications of Female Candidates? Examining Gender Bias in News Coverage across National and Local Newspapers. *Journalism & Mass Communication Quarterly*, *101*(3), 657–678. https://doi.org/10.1177/10776990221100514.

Bauer, N. M., & Cargile, I. A. (2023). Women Get the Job Done: Differences in Constituent Communication from Female and Male Lawmakers. *Politics & Gender*, *19*(4), 1110–1133. https://doi.org/10.1017/S1743923X23000259.

Bauer, N. M., & Santia, M. (2023, January). Gendered Times: How Gendered Contexts Shape Campaign Messages of Female Candidates. *Journal of Communication*, *73*(4), 329–341. https://doi.org/10.1093/joc/jqac052.

Bauer, N. M., & Taylor, T. (2023, March). Selling Them Short? Differences in News Coverage of Female and Male Candidate Qualifications. *Political Research Quarterly*, *76*(1), 308–322. https://doi.org/10.1177/10659129221086024.

Bejarano, C., & Smooth, W. (2022, January). Women of Color Mobilizing: Sistahs Are Doing It for Themselves from GOTV to Running Candidates for Political Office. *Journal of Women, Politics & Policy*, *43*(1), 8–24. https://doi.org/10.1080/1554477X.2022.2008398.

Beller, A. H. (1982). Occupational Segregation by Sex: Determinants and Changes. *Journal of Human Resources*, *17*(3), 371–392. https://doi.org/10.2307/145586.

Benjamin, A. (2023). PACs Rule Everything Around Me: How Political Action Committees Shape Elections and Policy in the Local Context. In S. Anzia (Ed.), *Interest Groups in U.S. Local Politics*. Cham: Palgrave Macmillan. https://doi.org/10.1007/978-3-031-37626-9_6.

Benjamin, A., & Miller, A. (2019). Picking Winners: How Political Organizations Influence Local Elections. *Urban Affairs Review*, *55*(3), 643–674. https://doi.org/10.1177/1078087417732647.

Bernhard, R. (2022). Wearing the Pants(suit)? Gendered Leadership Styles, Partisanship, and Candidate Evaluation in the 2016 U.S. Election. *Politics & Gender*, *18*(2), 513–545. https://doi.org/10.1017/S1743923X20000665

Bernhard, R., & de Benedictis-Kessner, J. (2021, June). Men and Women Candidates Are Similarly Persistent after Losing Elections. *Proceedings of the National Academy of Sciences*, *118*(26), e2026726118. https://doi.org/10.1073/pnas.2026726118.

Bernhard, R., Eggers, A., & Klašnja, M. (2024). *A Rich Woman's World? Wealth and Gendered Paths to Office*. [Working Paper].

Bernhard, R., & Freeder, S. (2020). The More You Know: Voter Heuristics and the Information Search. *Political Behavior*, *42*(2), 603–623. https://doi.org/10.1007/s11109-018-9512-2.

Bernhard, R., Shames, S., & Teele, D. L. (2021). To Emerge? Breadwinning, Motherhood, and Women's Decisions to Run for Office. *American Political Science Review, 115*(2), 379–394.

Bittner, A., & Goodyear-Grant, E. (2017, February). Sex Isn't Gender: Reforming Concepts and Measurements in the Study of Public Opinion. *Political Behavior, 39*(4), 1019–1041. https://doi.org/10.1007/s11109-017-9391-y.

Blackstone, A. M. (2003). Gender Roles and Society. *Journal of Marriage and the Family, 57*, 5–19.

Bonica, A. (2017). Professional Networks, Early Fundraising, and Electoral Success. *Election Law Journal, 16*(1), 153–171.

Bonica, A. (2020, May). Why Are There So Many Lawyers in Congress? *Legislative Studies Quarterly, 45*(2), 253–289. https://doi.org/10.1111/lsq.12265.

Borrowman, M., & Klasen, S. (2020, April). Drivers of Gendered Sectoral and Occupational Segregation in Developing Countries. *Feminist Economics, 26*(2), 62–94. https://doi.org/10.1080/13545701.2019.1649708.

Bos, A. L., Greenlee, J. S., Holman, M. R., Oxley, Z. M., & Lay, J. C. (2021). This One's for the Boys: How Gendered Political Socialization Limits Girls' Political Ambition and Interest. *American Political Science Review, 116*(2), 484–501. doi:10.1017/S0003055421001027.

Brown, N. E., & Gershon, S. A. (Eds.). (2016). *Distinct Identities: Minority Women in U.S. Politics*. New York: Routledge.

Budd, D., Myers, A., & Longoria, T. (2016). The Role of a Gendered Policy Agenda in Closing the Mayoral Ambition Gap: The Case of Texas Female City Council Members. *Journal of Research on Women and Gender, 6*, 81–93.

Bureau, U.S. Census. (2021). *Number of Women-Owned Employer Firms Increased 0.6% from 2017 to 2018* (Tech. Rep.). Author. www.census.gov/library/stories/2021/03/women-business-ownership-in-america-on-rise.html. (Section: Government)

Burnett, C. M. (2019, July). Parties as an Organizational Force on Nonpartisan City Councils. *Party Politics, 25*(4), 594–608. https://doi.org/10.1177/1354068817737996.

Burns, P. (2003). Regime Theory, State Government, and a Takeover of Urban Education. *Journal of Urban Affairs, 25*(3), 285–303. https://doi.org/10.1111/1467-9906.00163.

Burrell, B. (2014). *Gender in Campaigns for the US House of Representatives*. Ann Arbor: University of Michigan Press.

Busch, F. (2020). Gender Segregation, Occupational Sorting, and Growth of Wage Disparities between Women. *Demography, 57*(3), 1063–1088. https://doi.org/10.1007/s13524-020-00887-3.

Butler, D. M., & Preece, J. R. (2016, February). Recruitment and Perceptions of Gender Bias in Party Leader Support. *Political Research Quarterly*, *69*(4), 842–851. https://doi.org/10.1177/1065912916668412.

Campbell, R., & Cowley, P. (2014, February). Rich Man, Poor Man, Politician Man: Wealth Effects in a Candidate Biography Survey Experiment. *The British Journal of Politics and International Relations*, *16*(1), 56–74. https://doi.org/10.1111/1467-856X.12002.

Canary, D. J., Cunningham, E. M., & Cody, M. J. (1988). Goal Types, Gender, and Locus of Control in Managing Interpersonal Conflict. *Communication Research*, *15*(4), 426–446. https://doi.org/10.1177/009365088015004005.

Cargile, I. A. M. (2015). Latina Issues: An Analysis of the Policy Issue Competencies of Latina Candidates. In S. A. Gershon, & N. E. Brown (Eds.), *Distinct Identities: Minority Women in U.S. Politics.* (pp. 68–82) New York: Routledge.

Cargile, I. A. M., & Pringle, L. (2019, July). Context Not Candidate Sex: A Case Study of Female Vote Choice for Mayor. *Urban Affairs Review*, *56*(6), 1659–1686. https://doi.org/10.1177/1078087419861697.

Carmines, E. G., & Stimson, J. A. (1990). *Issue Evolution: Race and the Transformation of American Politics*. Princeton: Princeton University Press.

Carnes, N. (2018). *The Cash Ceiling: Why Only the Rich Run for Office–and What We Can Do about It*. Princeton: Princeton University Press.

Carroll, S. J., & Sanbonmatsu, K. (2013). Entering the Mayor's Office: Women's Decisions to Run for Municipal Positions. In M. Rose (Ed.), *Women and Executive Office: Pathways and Performance.* (pp. 101–114) Boulder, CO: Lynne Rienner.

Cassese, E. C. (2019). Partisan Dehumanization in American Politics. *Political Behavior*, *43*, 29–50. https://doi.org/10.1007/s11109-019-09545-w.

Cassese, E. C., & Holman, M. R. (2019). Playing the Woman Card: Ambivalent Sexism in the 2016 U.S. Presidential Race. *Political Psychology*, *40*(1), 55–74. https://doi.org/10.1111/pops.12492.

CAWP. (2019). *Current Numbers | CAWP*. https://www.cawp.rutgers.edu/current-numbers.

CAWP. (2020). *Women in State Legislative Leadership* (Tech. Rep.). Center for American Women and Politics, Eagleton Institute of Politics, Rutgers University.

Chambers-Ju, C. (2014, April). Data Collection, Opportunity Costs, and Problem Solving: Lessons from Field Research on Teachers' Unions in Latin America. *PS: Political Science & Politics*, *47*(2), 405–409. https://doi.org/10.1017/S1049096514000304.

Childs, S., & Hughes, M. (2018, June). 'Which Men?' How an Intersectional Perspective on Men and Masculinities Helps Explain Women's Political Underrepresentation. *Politics & Gender*, *14*(2), 282–287. https://doi.org/10.1017/S1743923X1800017X.

Claveria, S. (2014, September). Still a 'Male Business'? Explaining Women's Presence in Executive Office. *West European Politics*, *37*(5), 1156–1176. https://doi.org/10.1080/01402382.2014.911479.

Clayton, A., O'Brien, D. Z., & Piscopo, J. M. (2019). All Male Panels? Representation and Democratic Legitimacy. *American Journal of Political Science*, *63*(1), 113–129. Retrieved 10-10-2018, from https://onlinelibrary.wiley.com/doi/abs/10.1111/ajps.12391. https://doi.org/10.1111/ajps.12391.

Clayton, A., & Zetterberg, P. (2018). Quota Shocks: The Budgetary Implications of Electoral Gender Quotas Worldwide. *Journal of Politics*, *80*(3), 916–932. https://doi.org/10.1086/697251.

Coffé, H., & Theiss-Morse, E. (2016). The Effect of Political Candidates' Occupational Background on Voters' Perceptions of and Support for Candidates. *Political Science*, *68*(1), 55–77.

Cohen, A. K., & Hodges, H. M. (1963). Characteristics of the Lower-Blue-Collar-Class. *Social Problems*, *10*(4), 303–334. https://doi.org/10.2307/799204.

Cohen, P. N. (2013). The Persistence of Workplace Gender Segregation in the US. *Sociology Compass*, *7*(11), 889–899. https://doi/org/10.1111/soc4.12083.

Conroy, M. (2016). *Masculinity, Media, and the American Presidency*. New York: Springer.

Conroy, M., & Green, J. (2020, February). It Takes a Motive: Communal and Agentic Articulated Interest and Candidate Emergence. *Political Research Quarterly*, *73*(4), 942–956. https://doi.org/10.1177/1065912920933668.

Crawford, N. N. (2024). Marked Men: Black Politicians and the Racialization of Scandal. In *Marked Men*. New York: New York University Press.

Crenshaw, K. (1989). Demarginalizing the Intersection of Race and Sex. *University of Chicago Legal Forces*, *1989*(1), 139–168.

Crenshaw, K. (1991). Mapping the Margins: Intersectionality, Identity Politics, and Violence against Women of Color. *Stanford Law Review*, *43*(6), 1241–1299. www.jstor.org/stable/1229039.

Crowder-Meyer, M. (2013). Gendered Recruitment without Trying: How Local Party Recruiters Affect Women's Representation. *Politics & Gender*, *9*(4), 390–413. http://journals.cambridge.org/abstract_S1743923X13000391.

Crowder-Meyer, M. (2020). Baker, Bus Driver, Babysitter, Candidate? Revealing the Gendered Development of Political Ambition among Ordinary Americans. *Political Behavior*, *42*(359–384). https://doi.org/10.1007/s11109-018-9498-9.

Crowder-Meyer, M., & Cooperman, R. (2018). How Party Culture among Donors Contributes to the Party Gap in Women's Representation. *Journal of Politics*, *80*(4), 1211–1224. https://doi.org/10.1086/698848.

Crowder-Meyer, M., Gadarian, S. K., & Trounstine, J. (2015). Electoral Institutions, Gender Stereotypes, and Women's Local Representation. *Politics, Groups, and Identities*, *3*(2), 318–334. https://doi.org/10.1080/21565503.2015.1031803.

Crowder-Meyer, M., Gadarian, S. K., & Trounstine, J. (2019, February). Voting Can Be Hard, Information Helps. *Urban Affairs Review*, *56*(1), 124–153. https://doi.org/10.1177/1078087419831074.

Crowder-Meyer, M., & Lauderdale, B. E. (2014, April). A Partisan Gap in the Supply of Female Potential Candidates in the United States. *Research & Politics*, *1*(1), 2053168014537230. https://doi.org/10.1177/2053168014537230.

Cruz, C., Keefer, P., & Labonne, J. (2021). Buying Informed Voters: New effects of Information on Voters and Candidates. *The Economic Journal*, *131*(635), 1105–1134. https://doi.org/10.1093/ej/ueaa112.

Cruz, C., Labonne, J., & Querubín, P. (2017, October). Politician Family Networks and Electoral Outcomes: Evidence from the Philippines. *American Economic Review*, *107*(10), 3006–3037. https://doi.org/10.1257/aer.20150343.

Dahl, R. (1961). *Who Governs? Democracy and Power in an American City*. New Haven, CT: Yale University Press.

Davidson, A. M., McGregor, R. M., & Siemiatycky, M. (2020). Gender, Race and Political Ambition: The Case of Ontario School Board Elections. *Canadian Journal of Political Science/Revue canadienne de science politique*, *53*(2), 461–475. doi:10.1017/S0008423919001057.

Davis, M. J. (2007). The Battle over Implied Preemption: Products Liability and the FDA. *Boston College Law Review*, *48*, 1089.

de Benedictis-Kessner, J. (2017, December). Off-Cycle and Out of Office: Election Timing and the Incumbency Advantage. *The Journal of Politics*, *80*(1), 119–132. https://doi.org/10.1086/694396.

de Benedictis-Kessner, J. (2018). How Attribution Inhibits Accountability: Evidence from Train Delays. *Journal of Politics*, *80*(4), 1417–1422. https://doi.org/10.1086/698754.

de Benedictis-Kessner, J., Einstein, K. L., & Palmer, M. (2023, June). *Who Should Make Decisions? Public Perceptions of Democratic Inclusion in Housing Policy* [SSRN Scholarly Paper]. Rochester, NY. https://doi.org/10.2139/ssrn.4487350.

de Benedictis-Kessner, J., Lee, D. D. I., Velez, Y. R., & Warshaw, C. (2023, December). American Local Government Elections Database. *Scientific Data*, *10*(1), 912. https://doi.org/10.1038/s41597-023-02792-x.

de Benedictis-Kessner, J., & Warshaw, C. (2016, August). Mayoral Partisanship and Municipal Fiscal Policy. *The Journal of Politics*, *78*(4), 1124–1138. https://doi.org/10.1086/686308.

de Benedictis-Kessner, J., & Warshaw, C. (2020a). Accountability for the Local Economy at All Levels of Government in United States Elections. *American Political Science Review*, *114.3*(2020), 660–676. https://doi.org/10.1017/S0003055420000027.

de Benedictis-Kessner, J., & Warshaw, C. (2020b). Politics in Forgotten Governments: The Partisan Composition of County Legislatures and County Fiscal Policies. *The Journal of Politics*, *82*(2), 460–475. https://doi.org/10.1086/706458.

Deckman, M. (2004). Women Running Locally: How Gender Affects School Board Elections. *PS: Political Science and Politics*, *37*(1), 61–62.

DeMora, S. L., Lindke, C. A., Merolla, J. L., & Stephenson, L. B. (2022, June). Ready for a Woman President?: Polls, Public Comfort, and Perceptions of Electability in the 2020 Democratic Nomination. *Public Opinion Quarterly*, *86*(2), 270–292. https://doi.org/10.1093/poq/nfac012.

DeWitt, D. (2021, August). Occupational Engagement and Partisanship in the United States. *Political Studies Review*, *19*(3), 501–510. https://doi.org/10.1177/1478929920932129.

Diekman, A. B., Brown, E. R., Johnston, A. M., & Clark, E. K. (2010, August). Seeking Congruity between Goals and Roles: A New Look at Why Women Opt Out of Science, Technology, Engineering, and Mathematics Careers. *Psychological Science*, *21*(8), 1051–1057. https://doi.org/10.1177/0956797610377342.

Diekman, A. B., Clark, E. K., Johnston, A. M., Brown, E. R., & Steinberg, M. (2011). Malleability in Communal Goals and Beliefs Influences Attraction to Stem Careers: Evidence for a Goal Congruity Perspective. *Journal of Personality and Social Psychology*, *101*(5), 902. https://doi.org/10.1037/a0025199.

Diekman, A. B., & Eagly, A. H. (2000). Stereotypes as Dynamic Constructs: Women and Men of the Past, Present, and Future. *Personality and*

Social Psychology Bulletin, *26*(10), 1171–1188. https://doi.org/10.1177/0146167200262001.

Diekman, A. B., & Goodfriend, W. (2006, February). Rolling with the Changes: A Role Congruity Perspective on Gender Norms. *Psychology of Women Quarterly*, *30*(4), 369–383. https://doi.org/10.1111/j.1471-6402.2006.00312.x.

Diekman, A. B., & Murnen, S. K. (2004, March). Learning to Be Little Women and Little Men: The Inequitable Gender Equality of Nonsexist Children's Literature. *Sex Roles*, *50*(5–6), 373–385. https://doi.org/10.1023/B:SERS.0000018892.26527.ea.

Eagly, A. H. (2007). Female Leadership Advantage and Disadvantage: Resolving the Contradictions. *Psychology of Women Quarterly*, *31*(1), 1–12. http://dx.doi.org/10.1111/j.1471-6402.2007.00326.x.

Eagly, A. H., & Karau, S. J. (2002). Role Congruity Theory of Prejudice toward Female Leaders. *Psychological Review*, *109*(3), 573–598. DOI: 10.1037/0033-295x.109.3.573.

Eagly, A. H., & Koenig, A. M. (2006). *Social Role Theory of Sex Differences and Similarities: Implication for Prosocial Behavior.* In D. J. Canary, & K. Dindia (Eds.), *Sex Differences and Similarities in Communication* (pp. 100–116). New York: Taylor Francis.

Eagly, A. H., Wood, W., & Diekman, A. B. (2000). Social Role Theory of Sex Differences and Similarities: A Current Appraisal. In T. Eckes, & H. M. Trautner (Eds.), *The Developmental Social Psychology of Gender* (pp. 123–174). New York: Psychology Press.

Einstein, K. L., Glick, D. M., Palmer, M., & Pressel, R. J. (2020). Do Mayors Run for Higher Office? New Evidence on Progressive Ambition. *American Politics Research*, *48*(1), 197–221. https://doi.org/10.1177/1532673X17752322.

Einstein, K. L., Palmer, M., & Glick, D. M. (2019). Who Participates in Local Government? Evidence from Meeting Minutes. *Perspectives on Politics*, *17*(1), 28–46. doi:10.1017/S153759271800213X.

Elsässer, L., & Schäfer, A. (2022, September). (N)one of Us? The Case for Descriptive Representation of the Contemporary Working Class. *West European Politics*, *45*(6), 1361–1384. https://doi.org/10.1080/01402382.2022.2031443.

Elsässer, L., & Schäfer, A. (2023). Political Inequality in Rich Democracies. *Annual Review of Political Science*, *26*(1), 469–487. https://doi.org/10.1146/annurev-polisci-052521-094617.

Evans, C. D., & Diekman, A. B. (2009, June). On Motivated Role Selection: Gender Beliefs, Distant Goals and Career Interest. *Psychology of*

Women Quarterly, *33*(2), 235–249. https://doi.org/10.1111/j.1471-6402.2009.01493.x.

Farris, E. M., & Holman, M. R. (2023a, September). Local Gun Safety Enforcement, Sheriffs, and Right-Wing Political Extremism. *Urban Affairs Review*. https://doi.org/10.1177/10780874231203681.

Farris, E. M., & Holman, M. R. (2023b). Sheriffs, Right-Wing Extremism, and the Limits of U.S. Federalism during a Crisis. *Social Science Quarterly*, *104*(2), 59–68. https://doi.org/10.1111/ssqu.13244.

Farris, E. M., & Holman, M. R. (2024). *The Power of the Badge*. Chicago, IL: University of Chicago Press.

Ferreira, F., & Gyourko, J. (2014, April). Does Gender Matter for Political Leadership? The Case of U.S. Mayors. *Journal of Public Economics*, *112*, 24–39. https://doi.org/10.1016/j.jpubeco.2014.01.006.

Fox, R. L., & Oxley, Z. M. (2003). Gender Stereotyping in State Executive Elections: Candidate Selection and Success. *The Journal of Politics*, *65*(3), 833–850. https://doi.org/10.1111/1468-2508.00214.

Fox, R. L., & Oxley, Z. M. (2004). Women in Executive Office: Variation across American States. *Political Research Quarterly*, *57*(1), 113–120. https://doi.org/10.1177/106591290405700109.

Fraga, B. L., Gonzalez Juenke, E., & Shah, P. (2020, April). One Run Leads to Another: Minority Incumbents and the Emergence of Lower Ticket Minority Candidates. *The Journal of Politics*, *82*(2), 771–775. https://doi.org/10.1086/706599.

Friedman, S., & Laurison, D. (2019). *The Class Ceiling: Why It Pays to Be Priviledged*. Bristol: Policy Press.

Friedman, S., Laurison, D., & Miles, A. (2015, May). Breaking the 'Class' Ceiling? Social Mobility into Britain's Elite Occupations. *The Sociological Review*, *63*(2), 259–289. https://doi.org/10.1111/1467-954X.12283.

Friesen, A., & Holman, M. R. (2022, June). Racial Limitations on the Gender, Risk, Religion, and Politics Model. *Politics and Religion*, *15*(2), 270–290. https://doi.org/10.1017/S1755048321000250.

Fujishiro, K., Xu, J., & Gong, F. (2010, December). What Does 'Occupation' Represent as an Indicator of Socioeconomic Status?: Exploring Occupational Prestige and Health. *Social Science & Medicine*, *71*(12), 2100–2107. https://doi.org/10.1016/j.socscimed.2010.09.026.

Fulton, S. A., Maestas, C. D., Maisel, L. S., & Stone, W. J. (2006). The Sense of a Woman: Gender, Ambition, and the Decision to Run for Congress. *Political Research Quarterly*, *59*(2), 235–248. https://doi.org/10.1177/106591290605900206

Funk, K. D. (2015, September). Gendered Governing? Women's Leadership Styles and Participatory Institutions in Brazil. *Political Research Quarterly*, *68*(3), 564–578. https://doi.org/10.1177/1065912915589130.

Funk, K. D., & Molina, A. L. (2022). Closing the Gap: How Mayors' Individual Attributes Affect Gender Wage Disparities in Local Bureaucracies. *Review of Public Personnel Administration*, *42*(3), 553–573. https://doi.org/10.1177/0734371X211002610.

Funk, K. D., & Philips, A. Q. (2019). Representative Budgeting: Women Mayors and the Composition of Spending in Local Governments. *Political Research Quarterly*, *72*(1), 19–33. https://doi.org/10.1177/1065912918775237.

Gallup (2022, January). *Military Brass, Judges among Professions at New Image Lows.* Retrieved 05-10-2023, from https://news.gallup.com/poll/388649/military-brass-judges-among-professions-new-image-lows.aspx. (Section: Politics)

Gilens, M. (2012). *Affluence and Influence: Economic Inequality and Political Power in America*. Princeton: Princeton University Press. https://doi.org/10.1515/9781400844821.

Gingrich, J., & Häusermann, S. (2015). The Decline of the Working-Class Vote, the Reconfiguration of the Welfare Support Coalition and Consequences for the Welfare State. *Journal of European Social Policy*, *25*(1), 50–75. https://doi.org/10.1177/0958928714556970.

Goldin, C. (2021, October). Career and Family: Women's Century-Long Journey toward Equity. In *Career and Family*. Princeton University Press. https://doi.org/10.1515/9780691226736.

Gould, M. (1977). Toward a Sociological Theory of Gender and Sex. *The American Sociologist*, *12*(4), 182–189. Retrieved 08-06-2023, from https://www.jstor.org/stable/27702297.

Greenberg, E. S., Grunberg, L., & Daniel, K. (1996, June). Industrial Work and Political Participation: Beyond 'Simple Spillover'. *Political Research Quarterly*, *49*(2), 305–330. https://doi.org/10.1177/106591299604900204.

Group, I. (2023). *New Education Analysis about District Superintendency* Retrieved 27-01-2024, from www.ilogroup.com/research/new-education-analysis-about-district-superintendency/.

Grumbach, J. M. (2015, June). Does the American Dream Matter for Members of Congress?: Social-Class Backgrounds and Roll-Call Votes. *Political Research Quarterly*, *68*(2), 306–323. https://doi.org/10.1177/1065912915572902.

Grumbach, J. M., Sahn, A., & Staszak, S. (2020). Gender, Race, and Intersectionality in Campaign Finance. *Political Behavior*, *44*, 319–340 (2022). https://doi.org/10.1007/s11109-020-09619-0.

Gunderson, A., Cohen, E., Schiff, K. J., et al. (2021). Counterevidence of Crime-Reduction Effects from Federal Grants of Military Equipment to Local Police. *Nature Human Behaviour*, *5*(2), 194–204. https://doi.org/10.1038/s41562-020-00995-5.

Guy, M. E., & Newman, M. A. (2004). Women's Jobs, Men's Jobs: Sex Segregation and Emotional Labor. *Public Administration Review*, *64*(3), 289–298. http://dx.doi.org/10.1111/j.1540-6210.2004.00373.x.

Hait, A. (2021, March). *Number of Women-Owned Employer Firms Increased 0.6% from 2017 to 2018* (Tech. Rep.). US Census Bureau. Retrieved 24-01-2024, from www.census.gov/library/stories/2021/03/women-business-ownership-in-america-on-rise.html. (Section: Government)

Hajnal, Z., & Trounstine, J. (2014, January). What Underlies Urban Politics? Race, Class, Ideology, Partisanship, and the Urban Vote. *Urban Affairs Review*, *50*(1), 63–99. https://doi.org/10.1177/1078087413485216.

Hankinson, M., & Magazinnik, A. (2023). *Districting without Parties: How City Council Maps Increase Minority Representation* [Working paper]. Retrieved 04-01-2024, from https://files.osf.io/v1/resources/vt3bk/providers/osfstorage/6492fe60a2a2f404d9436b4a?action=download&direct&version=1.

Hartney, M. T. (2023). Teachers' Unions and School Board Elections: A Reassessment. In S. Anzia (Ed.), *Interest Groups in U.S. Local Politics* (pp. 59–84). https://doi.org/10.1007/978-3-031-37626-9_4.

He, J. C., Kang, S. K., Tse, K., & Toh, S. M. (2019). Stereotypes at Work: Occupational Stereotypes Predict Race and Gender Segregation in the Workforce. *Journal of Vocational Behavior*, *115*, 103318. https://doi.org/10.1016/j.jvb.2019.103318.

Heerde, J. V., & Bowler, S. (2007, July). Parties in an Anti–party State: The Case of California. *Journal of Elections, Public Opinion and Parties*, *17*(2), 143–163. https://doi.org/10.1080/13689880701348878.

Hirschman, A. O. (1970). *Exit, Voice, and Loyalty: Responses to Decline in Firms, Organizations, and States*. Cambridge, MA: Harvard University Press.

Hochschild, A., & Machung, A. (2012). *The Second Shift: Working Families and the Revolution at Home*. New York: Penguin.

Holman, M. R. (2014, October). Sex and the City: Female Leaders and Spending on Social Welfare Programs in U.S. Municipalities. *Journal of Urban Affairs*, 36(4), 701–715. https://doi.org/10.1111/juaf.12066.

Holman, M. R. (2015). *Women in Politics in the American City*. Philadelphia, PA: Temple University Press.

Holman, M. R. (2016a). The Differential Effect of Resources on Political Participation across Gender and Racial Groups. In N. E. Brown, & S. A. Gershon (Eds.), *Distinct Identities: Minority Women in U.S. Politics* (pp. 64–86). New York: Routledge.

Holman, M. R. (2016b). Gender, Political Rhetoric, and Moral Metaphors in State of the City Addresses. *Urban Affairs Review*, 52(4), 501–530. https://doi.org/10.1177/1078087415589191.

Holman, M. R. (2017, December). Women in Local Government: What We Know and Where We Go from Here. *State and Local Government Review*, 49(4), 285–296. https://doi.org/10.1177/0160323X17732608.

Holman, M. R. (2023, January). Gender Stereotyping Questions Accurately Measure Beliefs about the Traits and Issue Strengths of Women and Men in Politics. *Journal of Women, Politics & Policy*, 44(1), 90–104. https://doi.org/10.1080/1554477X.2023.2162285.

Holman, M. R., & Lay, J. C. (2021, March). Are You Picking Up What I Am Laying Down? Ideology in Low-Information Elections. *Urban Affairs Review*, 57(2), 315–341. https://doi.org/10.1177/1078087420908933.

Holman, M. R., & Mahoney, A. M. (2018). Stop, Collaborate, and Listen: Women's Collaboration in US State Legislatures. *Legislative Studies Quarterly*, 43(2), 179–206. https://doi.org/10.1111/lsq.12199.

Holman, M. R., Mahoney, A. M., & Hurler, E. (2021). Let's Work Together: Bill Success via Women's Cosponsorship in U.S. State Legislatures. *Political Research Quarterly*. https://doi.org/https://doi.org/10.1177/10659129211020123.

Holman, M. R., Merolla, J. L., & Zechmeister, E. J. (2017, January). Can Experience Overcome Stereotypes in Times of Terror Threat? *Research & Politics*, 4(1), 2053168016688121. https://doi.org/10.1177/2053168016688121.

Holman, M. R., Merolla, J. L., & Zechmeister, E. J. (2022, February). The Curious Case of Theresa May and the Public that Did Not Rally: Gendered Reactions to Terrorist Attacks Can Cause Slumps Not Bumps. *American Political Science Review*, 116(1), 249–264. https://doi.org/10.1017/S0003055421000861.

Holman, M. R., Merolla, J. L., Zechmeister, E. J., & Wang, D. (2019). Terrorism, Gender, and the 2016 Presidential Election . *Electoral Studies*, *61(1)*, 102033. https://doi.org/10.1016/j.electstud.2019.03.009

Holman, M. R., & Schneider, M. C. (2018). Gender, Race, and Political Ambition: How Intersectionality and Frames Influence Interest in Political Office. *Politics, Groups, and Identities*, *6*(2), 264–280. https://doi.org/10.1080/21565503.2016.1208105.

hooks, b. (2014). Sisterhood: Political Solidarity between Women. In *Feminist Social Thought* (pp. 484–500). New York: Routledge.

Hopkins, D. J., & Pettingill, L. M. (2018, October). Retrospective Voting in Big-City US Mayoral Elections. *Political Science Research and Methods*, *6*(4), 697–714. https://doi.org/10.1017/psrm.2016.54.

Hopkins, D. J., & Williamson, T. (2012, March). Inactive by Design? Neighborhood Design and Political Participation. *Political Behavior*, *34*(1), 79–101. https://doi.org/10.1007/s11109-010-9149-2.

Huddy, L., & Terkildsen, N. (1993). The Consequences of Gender Stereotypes for Women Candidates at Different Levels and Types of Office. *Political Research Quarterly*, *46*(3), 503–525. https://doi.org/10.1177/106591299304600304.

Hunter, F. (1953). *Community Power Structure: A Study of Decision Makers*. Chapel Hill, NC: UNC Press Books.

Ingalls, G. L., & Arrington, T. S. (1991, June). The Role of Gender in Local Campaign Financing: The Case of Charlotte, North Carolina. *Women & Politics*, *11*(2), 61–89. https://doi.org/10.1300/J014v11n02_04.

Iversen, T., & Rosenbluth, F. (2008). Work and Power: The Connection between Female Labor Force Participation and Female Political Representation. *Annual Review of Political Science*, *11*(1), 479–495. https://doi.org/10.1146/annurev.polisci.11.053106.151342.

Iversen, T., & Rosenbluth, F. (2013). The Political Economy of Gender in Service Sector Economies. In A. Wren (Ed.), *The Political Economy of the Service Transition* (pp. 306–326). New York: Oxford University Press.

Jardina, A., & Piston, S. (2019). Racial Prejudice, Racial Identity, and Attitudes in Political Decision Making. In *Oxford Research Encyclopedia of Politics*. New York: Oxford University Press.

Jenkins, C. (2006). Women in Australian Politics: Mothers Only Need Apply. *Pacific Journalism Review*, *12*(1), 54.

Kalmijn, M. (1994). Assortative Mating by Cultural and Economic Occupational Status. *American Journal of Sociology*, *100*(2), 422–452. https://doi.org/10.1086/230542.

Kam, C.D., & Zechmeister, E.J. (2013, October). Name Recognition and Candidate Support. *American Journal of Political Science*, 57(4), 971–986. https://doi.org/10.1111/ajps.12034.

Kanthak, K., & Woon, J. (2015). Women Don't Run? Election Aversion and Candidate Entry. *American Journal of Political Science*, 59(3), 595–612. https://doi.org/10.1111/ajps.12158.

Karpowitz, C. F., Monson, J. Q., & Preece, J. R. (2017). How to Elect More Women: Gender and Candidate Success in a Field Experiment. *American Journal of Political Science*, 61(4), 927–943. https://doi.org/10.1111/ajps.12300.

Keele, L. J., Shah, P. R., White, I., & Kay, K. (2017, July). Black Candidates and Black Turnout: A Study of Viability in Louisiana Mayoral Elections. *The Journal of Politics*, 79(3), 780–791. https://doi.org/10.1086/690302.

Kellogg, L. D., Gourrier, A. G., Bernick, E. L., & Brekken, K. (2019, January). County Governing Boards: Where Are All the Women? *Politics, Groups, and Identities*, 7(1), 39–51. https://doi.org/10.1080/21565503.2017.1304223.

Kettler, J. (2020). Paying It Forward: Candidate Contributions and Support for Diverse Candidates. In S. Shames, R. Bernhard, M. R. Holman, & D. L. Teele (Eds.), *Good Reasons to Run: Women and Political Candidacy* (pp. 114–121). Philadelphia, PA: Temple University Press.

Kettler, J. J. (2020, February). Buying Their Way In: Redistribution of Campaign Resources as a Path to State Legislative Leadership for Women. *The Social Science Journal*, 59(3), 341–356. https://doi.org/10.1080/03623319.2020.1727219.

Kim, H. J., & Kweon, Y. (2024). *Double Penalty? Examining the Class Effects of Gender Representation. Research & Politics*, 11(1), 20531680241226511. https://doi.org/10.1177/20531680241226511.

Kim, J. H., Kuk, J., & Kweon, Y. (2024, January). Did Low-Income Essential Workers during COVID-19 Increase Public Support for Redistribution? *Policy & Politics*, 1–23. https://doi.org/10.1332/03055736Y2023D000000008.

Kim, Y. (2019). Limits of Property Taxes and Charges: City Revenue Structures after the Great Recession. *Urban Affairs Review*, 55(1), 185–209.

Kim, Y., & Weseley, A. J. (2017). The Effect of Teacher Gender and Gendered Traits on Perceptions of Elementary School Teachers. *Journal of Research in Education*, 27(1), 114–133. Retrieved 25-09-2023, from https://eric.ed.gov/?id=EJ1142365.

Kirkland, P. A. (2020, March). Mayoral Candidates, Social Class, and Representation in American Cities. *Journal of Political Institutions and Political Economy*, 1(1), 105–136. https://doi.org/10.1561/112.00000004.

Kirkland, P. A. (2021, October). Business Owners and Executives as Politicians: The Effect on Public Policy. *The Journal of Politics*, 83(4), 1652–1668. https://doi.org/10.1086/715067.

Kirkland, P. A. (2022). Representation in American Cities: Who Runs for Mayor and Who Wins? *Urban Affairs Review*, 58(3), 635–670. https://doi.org/10.1177/10780874211021688.

Kitschelt, H., & Rehm, P. (2014, October). Occupations as a Site of Political Preference Formation. Comparative Political Studies, 47(12), 1670–1706. https://doi.org/10.1177/0010414013516066.

Kjelsrud, A., & Kotsadam, A. (2023). Female Employment and Voter Turnout: Evidence from India. *The Journal of Politics*, 85(4), 1569–1574. https://doi.org/10.1086/724966.

Koenig, A. M., Eagly, A. H., Mitchell, A. A., & Ristikari, T. (2011). Are Leader Stereotypes Masculine? A Meta-Analysis of Three Research Paradigms. *Psychological Bulletin*, 137(4), 616–642. https://doi.org/10.1037/a0023557.

Krebs, T. B., & Turner, F. S. (2015, May). Following the Money: The Influence of Campaign Finance Reform in the 2011 Chicago Mayoral Election. Journal of Urban Affairs, 37(2), 109–121. https://doi.org/10.1111/juaf.12099.

Kreiss, D., Lawrence, R. G., & McGregor, S. C. (2020, April). Political Identity Ownership: Symbolic Contests to Represent Members of the Public. *Social Media + Society*, 6(2), 2056305120926495. https://doi.org/10.1177/2056305120926495.

Kreitzer, R. J., & Osborn, T. (2019). The Emergence and Activities of Women's Recruiting Groups in the U.S. *Politics, Groups, and Identities*, 7(4), 842–852. https://doi.org/10.1080/21565503.2018.1531772.

Kreitzer, R. J., & Watts, C. S. (2018). Reproducible and Replicable: An Empirical Assessment of the Social Construction of Politically Relevant Target Groups. *PS: Political Science & Politics*, 51(4), 768–774. doi:10.1017/S1049096518000987.

Kroeber, C., & Hüffelmann, J. (2022, September). It's a Long Way to the Top: Women's Ministerial Career Paths. *Politics & Gender*, 18(3), 741–767. https://doi.org/10.1017/S1743923X21000118.

Kweon, Y. (2024). We See Symbols but Not Saviors: Women's Representation and the Political Attitudes of Working-Class Women. *Political Psychology*, OnlineFirst. https://doi.org/10.1111/pops.12953.

Lake, D. (2020, August). Nurses: Call to Action to Run for an Elected Office, Lessons from a State Senate Candidate. *JONA: The Journal of Nursing Administration*, 50(7/8), 372. https://doi.org/10.1097/NNA.0000000000000902.

Latura, A., & Weeks, A. C. (2023). Corporate Board Quotas and Gender Equality Policies in the Workplace. *American Journal of Political Science, 67*(3), 606–622. https://doi.org/10.1111/ajps.12709.

Lay, J. C. (2022). *Public Schools, Private Governance: Education Reform and Democracy in New Orleans*. Philadelphia, PA: Temple University Press.

Lay, J. C., Holman, M. R., Bos, A. L., et al. (2021). TIME for Kids to Learn Gender Stereotypes: Analysis of Gender and Political Leadership in a Common Social Studies Resource for Children. *Politics & Gender, 17*(1), 1–22. doi:10.1017/S1743923X19000540.

Lay, J. C., & Tyburski, M. D. (2017). The Buck Stops with the Education Mayor: Mayoral Control and Local Test Scores in U.S. Urban Mayoral Elections. *Politics & Policy, 45*(6), 964–1002. https://doi.org/10.1111/polp.12217.

Lazarus, J., & Steigerwalt, A. (2018). *Gendered Vulnerability*. Ann Arbor: University of Michigan Press.

Lee, S. W., & Mao, X. (2023, January). Recruitment and Selection of Principals: A Systematic Review. *Educational Management Administration & Leadership, 51*(1), 6–29. https://doi.org/10.1177/1741143220969694.

Leppert, R. (2023). *A Look at Black-Owned Businesses in the U.S.* (Tech. Rep.). Pew Research Center. Retrieved 24-01-2024, from www.pewresearch.org/short-reads/2023/02/21/a-look-at-black-owned-businesses-in-the-u-s/.

Levanon, A., England, P., & Allison, P. (2009). Occupational Feminization and Pay: Assessing Causal Dynamics Using 1950–2000 US Census Data. *Social Forces, 88*(2), 865–891. https://doi.org/10.1353/sof.0.0264.

Levanon, A., & Grusky, D. B. (2016, September). The Persistence of Extreme Gender Segregation in the Twenty-First Century. *American Journal of Sociology, 122*(2), 573–619. https://doi.org/10.1086/688628.

Lynd, R. S., & Lynd, H. M. (1929). *Middletown; a Study in Contemporary American Culture*. New York: Harcourt, Brace.

Lyness, K. S., & Grotto, A. R. (2018). Women and Leadership in the United States: Are We Closing the Gender Gap? *Annual Review of Organizational Psychology and Organizational Behavior, 5*, 227–265. https://doi.org/10.1146/annurev-orgpsych-032117-104739.

Lyon, M. A., Hemphill, A. A., & Jacobsen, R. (2022, October). How Do Unions Create Candidates? *Political Behavior*. https://doi.org/10.1007/s11109-022-09818-x.

Mansbridge, J. (2015, June). Should Workers Represent Workers? *Swiss Political Science Review, 21*(2), 261–270. https://doi.org/10.1111/spsr.12160.

Marschall, M., Shah, P., & Ruhil, A. (2011, January). The Study of Local Elections: Editors' Introduction: A Looking Glass into the Future. *PS: Political Science & Politics*, *44*(1), 97–100. https://doi.org/10.1017/S1049096510001940.

Martinez, M. (2023, January). 'You Can't Be a Teacher and Not Follow Politics!': Teacher-Legislators and Their Pathway to the State Capital. *Urban Education*, *58*(9), 2003–2030. https://doi.org/10.1177/0042085920926235.

Mastracci, S. H. (2004). *Breaking Out of the Pink-Collar Ghetto: Policy Solutions for Non-college Women*. New York: Routledge.

Matson, M., & Fine, T. S. (2006). Gender, Ethnicity, and Ballot Information: Ballot Cues in Low-Information Elections. *State Politics & Policy Quarterly*, *6*(1), 49–72. www.jstor.org/stable/41289378.

McBrayer, M., & Williams, R. L. (2023). The Second Sex in the Second District: The Policy Effects of Electing Women to County Government. *Political Research Quarterly*, *76*(2), 825–840. https://doi.org/10.1177/10659129221109144.

McDermott, M. (1997). Voting Cues in Low Information Elections: Candidate Gender as a Social Information Variable in Contemporary United States Elections. *American Journal of Political Science*, *41*(1), 270–283. https://doi.org/10.2307/2111716.

McDermott, M. (2005). Candidate Occupations and Voter Information Shortcuts. *The Journal of Politics*, *67*(1), 201–219. www.jstor.org/stable/3449711.

McDermott, M., & Panagopoulos, C. (2015, June). Be All that You Can Be: The Electoral Impact of Military Service as an Information Cue. *Political Research Quarterly*, *68*(2), 293–305. https://doi.org/10.1177/1065912915572151.

McGregor, R. M., Moore, A., Jackson, S., Bird, K., & Stephenson, L. B. (2017, April). Why So Few Women and Minorities in Local Politics?: Incumbency and Affinity Voting in Low Information Elections. *Representation*, *53*(2), 135–152. https://doi.org/10.1080/00344893.2017.1354909.

McGregor, S. C., & Mourão, R. R. (2016). Talking Politics on Twitter: Gender, Elections, and Social Networks. *Social Media+ Society*, *2*(3), https://doi.org/10.1177/2056305116664218.

McPherson, M., Smith-Lovin, L., & Cook, J. M. (2001, August). Birds of a Feather: Homophily in Social Networks. *Annual Review of Sociology*, *27*(1), 415–444. https://doi.org/10.1146/annurev.soc.27.1.415.

Mechtel, M. (2014, March). It's the Occupation, Stupid! Explaining Candidates' Success in Low-Information Elections. *European Journal of Political Economy*, *33*, 53–70. https://doi.org/10.1016/j.ejpoleco.2013.11.008.

Meeks, L. (2012). Is She 'Man Enough'? Women Candidates, Executive Political Offices, and News Coverage. *Journal of Communication, 62*(1), 175–193. https://doi.org/10.1111/j.1460-2466.2011.01621.x.

Moe, T. M., & Wiborg, S. (2016). *The Comparative Politics of Education: Teachers Unions and Education Systems around the World.* New York: Cambridge University Press.

Molotch, H. L. (1976, September). The City as a Growth Machine: Toward a Political Economy of Place. *American Journal of Sociology, 82*(2), 309–332. Retrieved 31-12-2014, from www.jstor.org/stable/2777096.

Murray, R. (2014). Quotas for Men: Reframing Gender Quotas as a Means of Improving Representation for All. *American Political Science Review, 108*(3), 520–532. https://doi.org/10.1017/S0003055414000239.

Murray, R. (2023). It's a Rich Man's World: How Class and Glass Ceilings Intersect for UK Parliamentary Candidates. *International Political Science Review, 44*(1), 13–26. https://doi.org/10.1177/01925121211040025.

Murray, S. B. (1996, August). 'WE ALL LOVE CHARLES': Men in Child Care and the Social Construction of Gender. *Gender & Society, 10*(4), 368–385. https://doi.org/10.1177/089124396010004002.

Muñoz, J., Anduiza, E., & Gallego, A. (2016). Why Do Voters Forgive Corrupt Mayors? Implicit Exchange, Credibility of Information and Clean Alternatives. *Local Government Studies, 42*(4), 598–615. https://doi.org/10.1080/03003930.2016.1154847.

Nordin, M. (2014). Do Voters Vote in Line with Their Policy Preferences? – The Role of Information. *CESifo Economic Studies, 60*(4), 681–721. https://doi.org/10.1093/cesifo/ifu012.

Norris, P., & Lovenduski, J. (1995). *Political Recruitment: Gender, Race and Class in the British Parliament.* New York: Cambridge University Press.

NSBA. (2020, October). *Gender Gap at the Top* (Tech. Rep.). National School Board Association. Retrieved 27-01-2024, from www.nsba.org:443/ASBJ/2020/October/gender-gap-top.

Ocampo, A. X. (2018, March). The Wielding Influence of Political Networks: Representation in Majority-Latino Districts. *Political Research Quarterly, 71*(1), 184–198. https://doi.org/10.1177/1065912917727368.

Ohmura, T., & Bailer, S. (2023, July). Power-Seeking, Networking and Competition: Why Women Do Not Rise in Parties. *West European Politics, 46*(5), 897–927. https://doi.org/10.1080/01402382.2022.2097442.

Okafor, C. O. (2017). Personality and Politics in Nigeria: A Psychological Exploration of the Agentic Theory of Political Participation. *Afro Asian Journal of Social Sciences, 8*(2), 1–18.

Oliver, S., & Conroy, M. (2018, January). Tough Enough for the Job? How Masculinity Predicts Recruitment of City Council Members. *American Politics Research*, *46*(6), 1094–1122. https://doi.org/10.1177/1532673X17729719.

Oliver, S., & Conroy, M. (2020). *Who Runs? The Masculine Advantage in Candidate Emergence*. Ann Arbor: University of Michigan Press.

Omi, M., & Winant, H. (2014). *Racial Formation in the United States*. Routledge.

Ondercin, H. L. (2022, February). Location, Location, Location: How Electoral Opportunities Shape Women's Emergence as Candidates. *British Journal of Political Science*, *52*(4), 1523–1543. https://doi.org/10.1017/S0007123421000508.

Osborn, T. (2012). *How Women Represent Women: Political Parties, Gender and Representation in the State Legislatures*. New York: Oxford University Press.

O'Grady, T. (2019, March). Careerists versus Coal-Miners: Welfare Reforms and the Substantive Representation of Social Groups in the British Labour Party. *Comparative Political Studies*, *52*(4), 544–578. https://doi.org/10.1177/0010414018784065.

Paxton, P. (2000). Women's Suffrage in the Measurement of Democracy: Problems of Operationalization. *Studies in Comparative International Development*, *35*(3), 92–111. https://doi.org/10.1007/BF02699767.

Peck, J. (2012). Austerity Urbanism: American Cities under Extreme Economy. *City*, *16*(6), 626–655. https://doi.org/10.1080/13604813.2012.734071.

Peterson, P. E. (1981). *City Limits*. Chicago: University of Chicago Press.

Pitkin, H. F. (1967). *The Concept of Representation*. Berkeley: University of California Press.

Preece, J. R. (2016). Mind the Gender Gap: An Experiment on the Influence of Self-Efficacy on Political Interest. *Politics & Gender*, *12*(1), 198–217. doi:10.1017/S1743923X15000628.

Preece, J. R., & Stoddard, O. B. (2015). Why Women Don't Run: Experimental Evidence on Gender Differences in Political Competition Aversion. *Journal of Economic Behavior & Organization*, *117*, 296–308. https://doi.org/10.1016/j.jebo.2015.04.019.

Preece, J. R., Stoddard, O. B., & Fisher, R. (2016). Run, Jane, Run! Gendered Responses to Political Party Recruitment. *Political Behavior*, *38*(3), 561–577. https://doi.org/10.1007/s11109-015-9327-3

Razzu, G., & Singleton, C. (2018, October). Segregation and Gender Gaps in the United Kingdom's Great Recession and Recovery. *Feminist Economics*, *24*(4), 31–55. https://doi.org/10.1080/13545701.2018.1451907.

Roos, P. A., & Reskin, B. F. (1984). Institutional Factors Contributing to Sex Segregation in the Workplace. *Sex Segregation in the Workplace: Trends, Explanations, Remedies*, 235–260.

Rosenbluth, F., Light, M., & Schrag, C. (2004, September). The Politics of Gender Equality. *Women & Politics*, *26*(2), 1–25. https://doi.org/10.1300/J014v26n02_01.

Royster, D. A. (2003). *Race and the Invisible Hand: How White Networks Exclude Black Men from Blue-Collar Jobs*. Berkeley: University of California Press.

Rubin, I. S., & Rubin, H. J. (1987, September). Economic Development Incentives: The Poor (Cities) Pay More. *Urban Affairs Quarterly*, *23*(1), 37–62. https://doi.org/10.1177/004208168702300104.

Rudman, L. A., & Phelan, J. E. (2008). Backlash Effects for Disconfirming Gender Stereotypes in Organizations. *Research in Organizational Behavior*, *28*, 61–79. https://doi.org/10.1016/j.riob.2008.04.003.

Sanbonmatsu, K. (2006, September). Gender Pools and Puzzles: Charting a Path to the Legislature. *Politics & Gender*, *1*(3), 387–400. doi:10.1017/S1743923X06251080.

Sances, M. W. (2017, July). Ideology and Vote Choice in U.S. Mayoral Elections: Evidence from Facebook Surveys. *Political Behavior*, 1–26. https://doi.org/10.1007/s11109-017-9420-x.

Sances, M. W. (2021). Do District Attorneys Represent Their Voters? Evidence from California's Era of Criminal Justice Reform. *Journal of Political Institutions and Political Economy*, *2*(2), 169–197. http://dx.doi.org/10.1561/113.00000034.

Sawicki, E. (2022, August). Rent Control Board Race All but Sewn Up. *Santa Monica Daily Press*. Retrieved 06-11-2023, from http://smdp.com/2022/08/29/rent-control-board-race-all-but-sewn-up/.

Saxton, G. W., & Barnes, T. D. (2022, January). Sex and Corruption in Congress: How the Nature of the Scandal Shapes Backlash from Voters. In M. J. Pomante (Ed.), *Scandal and Corruption in Congress* (pp. 193–212). Emerald. https://doi.org/10.1108/978-1-80117-119-920221017.

Schaffner, B. F., & Streb, M. J. (2002, February). The Partisan Heuristic in Low-Information Elections. *Public Opinion Quarterly*, *66*(4), 559–581. https://doi.org/10.1086/343755.

Schein, V. E., & Davidson, M. J. (1993). Think Manager, Think Male. *Management Development Review*, *6*(3). https://doi.org/10.1108/EUM0000000000738.

Schlozman, K. L., Burns, N., & Verba, S. (1999). 'What Happened at Work Today?': A Multistage Model of Gender, Employment, and Political Participation. *The Journal of Politics*, *61*(1), 29–53. https://doi.org/10.2307/2647774.

Schneider, M. C., & Bos, A. L. (2014). Measuring Stereotypes of Female Politicians. *Political Psychology*, *35*(2), 245–266. https://doi.org/10.1111/pops.12040.

Schneider, M. C., & Bos, A. L. (2019). The Application of Social Role Theory to the Study of Gender in Politics. *Political Psychology*, *40*(S1), 173–213. https://doi.org/10.1111/pops.12573.

Schneider, M. C., Bos, A. L., & DiFilippo, M. (2022, April). Gender Role Violations and Voter Prejudice: The Agentic Penalty Faced by Women Politicians. *Journal of Women, Politics & Policy*, *43*(2), 117–133. https://doi.org/10.1080/1554477X.2021.1981095.

Schneider, M. C., Holman, M. R., Diekman, A. B., & McAndrew, T. (2016). Power, Conflict, and Community: How Gendered Views of Political Power Influence Women's Political Ambition. *Political Psychology*, *37*(4), 515–531. https://doi.org/10.1111/pops.12268.

Schneider, M. C., & Sweet-Cushman, J. (2020). Pieces of Women's Political Ambition Puzzle: Changing Perceptions of a Political Career with Campaign Training. In S. L. Shames, R. Bernhard, M. R. Holman, & D. L. Teele (Eds.), *Good Reasons to Run: Women and Political Candidacy* (pp. 22–45). Philadelphia, PA: Temple University Press.

Schwindt-Bayer, L. A. (2011, March). Women Who Win: Social Backgrounds, Paths to Power, and Political Ambition in Latin American Legislatures. *Politics & Gender*, *7*(1), 1–33. https://doi.org/10.1017/S1743923X10000541.

Scott, J. (2022). It's All about the Money: Understanding How Black Women Fund Their Campaigns. *PS: Political Science & Politics*, *55*(2), 297–300. doi:10.1017/S1049096521001505.

Scott, J., Brown, N., Frasure, L., & Pinderhughes, D. (2021, January). Destined to Run? The Role of Political Participation on Black Women's Decision to Run for Elected Office. *National Review of Black Politics*, *2*(1), 22–52. https://doi.org/10.1525/nrbp.2021.2.1.22.

Sczesny, S. (2003). A Closer Look Beneath the Surface: Various Facets of the Think-Manager–Think-Male Stereotype. *Sex roles*, *49*, 353–363. https://doi.org/10.1023/A:1025112204526.

Shah, P. R., Juenke, E. G., & Fraga, B. L. (2022, April). Here Comes Everybody: Using a Data Cooperative to Understand the New Dynamics of Representation. *PS: Political Science & Politics*, *55*(2), 300–302. https://doi.org/10.1017/S1049096521001542.

Shames, S. L., Bernhard, R., Holman, M. R., & Teele, D. L. (Eds.). (2020). *Good Reasons to Run*. Philadelphia, PA: Temple University Press.

Siklodi, N., Ie, K. W., & Allen, N. (2023, July). From Gender Equity to Gendered Assignments? Women and Cabinet Committees in Canada and the United Kingdom. *Government and Opposition*, 1–24. https://doi.org/10.1017/gov.2023.18.

Silva, A., & Skulley, C. (2019). Always Running: Candidate Emergence among Women of Color over Time. *Political Research Quarterly*, 72(2), 342–359. https://doi.org/10.1177/1065912918789289.

Sobel, R. (1993). From Occupational Involvement to Political Participation: An Exploratory Analysis. *Political Behavior*, 15(4), 339–353. https://www.jstor.org/stable/586462.

Sokoloff, N. J. (1992). *Black Women and White Women in the Professions: Occupational Segregation by Race and Gender, 1960–1980*. New York: Psychology Press. https://doi.org/10.4324/9781315866505.

Sorensen, A., & Chen, P. (2022). Identity in Campaign Finance and Elections: The Impact of Gender and Race on Money Raised in 2010–2018 U.S. House Elections. *Political Research Quarterly*, 75(3), 738–753. https://doi.org/10.1177/10659129211022846.

Stalsburg, B. L. (2010, September). Voting for Mom: The Political Consequences of Being a Parent for Male and Female Candidates. *Politics & Gender*, 6(3), 373–404. https://doi.org/10.1017/S1743923X10000309.

Stauffer, K. E. (2021). Public Perceptions of Women's Inclusion and Feelings of Political Efficacy. *American Political Science Review*, 115(4), 1226–1241. https://doi.org/10.1017/S0003055421000678.

Stone, C. N. (1989). *Regime Politics: Governing Atlanta, 1946–1988*. Lawrence: University of Kansas Press.

Sumner, J. L., Farris, E. M., & Holman, M. R. (2020). Crowdsourcing Reliable Local Data. *Political Analysis*, 28(2), 244–262. DOI: 10.1017/pan.2019.32

Sumsion, J. (2000, June). Negotiating Otherness: A Male Early Childhood Educator's Gender Positioning. *International Journal of Early Years Education*, 8(2), 129–140. https://www.tandfonline.com/action/showCitFormats?doi=10.1080/09669760050046174.

Sweet-Cushman, J. (2016). Gender, Risk Assessment, and Political Ambition. *Politics and the Life Sciences*, 35(2) 1–17. https://doi.org/10.1017/pls.2016.13.

Sweet-Cushman, J. (2020a, September). Gendered Legislative Effectiveness in State Legislatures. In N. M. Bauer (Ed.), *Politicking while Female the Political Lives of Women* (pp. 137–157). Baton Rouge, LA: LSU Press.

Sweet-Cushman, J. (2020b). Where Does the Pipeline Get Leaky? The Progressive Ambition of School Board Members and Personal and Political Network Recruitment. *Politics, Groups, and Identities*, *8*(4), 762–785. https://doi.org/10.1080/21565503.2018.1541417.

Sweet-Cushman, J. (2021). Legislative vs. Executive Political Offices: How Gender Stereotypes Can Disadvantage Women in Either Office. *Political Behavior*, *44*(1), 411–434. https://doi.org/10.1007/s11109-021-09721-x.

Sweet-Cushman, J. (2023). *Inspired Citizens: How Our Political Role Models Shape American Politics*. Philadelphia, PA: Temple University Press.

Sweet-Cushman, J., & Bauer, N. M. (2024, March). Intersectional Motherhood and Candidate Evaluations in the United States. *Politics & Gender*, 1–22. https://doi.org/10.1017/S1743923X24000059.

Swers, M. L., & Thomsen, D. M. (2020). Building a Campaign Donor Network: How Candidate Gender and Partisanship Impact the Campaign Money Chase. In S. L. Shames, R. Bernhard, M. R. Holman, & D. L. Teele (Eds.), *Good Reasons to Run* (pp. 239–257). Philadelphia, PA: Temple University Press.

Sánchez, J. C., & Licciardello, O. (2012). Gender Differences and Attitudes in Entrepreneurial Intentions: The Role of Career Choice. *Journal of Women's Entrepreneurship and Education*, (1–2), 7–27.

Teele, D. L., Kalla, J., & Rosenbluth, F. (2018, August). The Ties that Double Bind: Social Roles and Women's Underrepresentation in Politics. *American Political Science Review*, *112*(3), 525–541. https://doi.org/10.1017/S0003055418000217.

Thompson, D. (2022). How Partisan Is Local Law Enforcement? Evidence from Sheriff Cooperation with Immigration Authorities. *American Political Science Review*, *114*(1), 222–236. https://doi.org/10.1017/S0003055419000613.

Thomsen, D. M., & Sanders, B. K. (2020). Gender Differences in Legislator Responsiveness. *Perspectives on Politics*, *18*(4), 1017–1030. https://doi.org/10.1017/S1537592719003414.

Thomsen, D. M., & Swers, M. L. (2017). Which Women Can Run? Gender, Partisanship, and Candidate Donor Networks. *Political Research Quarterly*, *70*(2), 449–463. https://doi.org/10.1177/1065912917698044.

Thébaud, S. (2010). Gender and Entrepreneurship as a Career Choice: Do Self-Assessments of Ability Matter? *Social Psychology Quarterly*, *73*(3), 288–304. doi: 10.1177/0190272510377882.

Thébaud, S. (2015). Business as Plan B: Institutional Foundations of Gender Inequality in Entrepreneurship across 24 Industrialized Countries. *Administrative Science Quarterly*, *60*(4), 671–711. doi: 10.1177/0001839215591627.

Tiebout, C. M. (1956). A Pure Theory of Local Expenditures. *Journal of Political Economy*, *64*(5), 416–424. https://www.jstor.org/stable/1826343.

Tolley, E. (2011). Do Women 'Do Better' in Municipal Politics? Electoral Representation across Three Levels of Government. *Canadian Journal of Political Science/Revue canadienne de science politique*, *44*(3), 573–594. doi:10.10170S0008423911000503.

Tolley, E., Besco, R., & Sevi, S. (2022). Who Controls the Purse Strings? A Longitudinal Study of Gender and Donations in Canadian Politics. *Politics & Gender*, *18*(1), 244–272. doi:10.1017/S1743923X20000276.

Tolley, E., & Paquet, M. (2021). Gender, Municipal Party Politics, and Montreal's First Woman Mayor. *Canadian Journal of Urban Research*, *30*(1), 40–52. ISSN: 2371-0292.

Tomaskovic-Devey, D. (2019). *Poverty and Social Welfare in the United States*. New York: Routledge. https://doi.org/10.4324/9780429302787.

Trounstine, J. (2009, September). All Politics Is Local: The Reemergence of the Study of City Politics. *Perspectives on Politics*, *7*(3), 611–618. https://doi.org/10.1017/S1537592709990892.

Trounstine, J. (2010). Representation and Accountability in Cities. *Annual Review of Political Science*, *13*(1), 407–423. https://doi.org/10.1146/annurev.polisci.032808.150414.

Trounstine, J. (2013, March). Turnout and Incumbency in Local Elections. *Urban Affairs Review*, *49*(2), 167–189. https://doi.org/10.1177/1078087412463536.

Valentino, L. (2021, December). The Heterarchy of Occupational Status: Evidence for Diverse Logics of Prestige in the United States. *Sociological Forum*, *36*(S1), 1395–1418. https://doi.org/10.1111/socf.12762.

van Setten, M., Scheepers, P., & Lubbers, M. (2017, August). Support for Restrictive Immigration Policies in the European Union 2002–2013: The Impact of Economic Strain and Ethnic Threat for Vulnerable Economic Groups. *European Societies*, *19*(4), 440–465. https://doi.org/10.1080/14616696.2016.1268705.

van Staalduinen, B., & Zollinger, D. (2023). *Upward Mobility, Gender, and Progressive Politics* [Working paper].

Volden, C., Wiseman, A. E., & Wittmer, D. E. (2013). When Are Women More Effective Lawmakers than Men? *American Journal of Political Science*, *57*(2), 326–341. www.jstor.org/stable/23496600.

Wade, M. M. (2018). Targeting Teachers while Shielding Cops? The Politics of Punishing Enemies and Rewarding Friends in American State Collective Bargaining Reform Agendas. *Journal of Labor and Society*, *21*(2), 137–157. https://doi.org/10.1111/wusa.12338.

Werner, T., & Mayer, K. R. (2007). Public Election Funding, Competition, and Candidate Gender. *PS: Political Science & Politics, 40*(4), 661–667. DOI: 10.1017/S1049096507071053.

Winters, J. A. (2011). *Oligarchy.* Cambridge: Cambridge University Press.

Wolbrecht, C., & Campbell, D. E. (2007). Leading by Example. *American Journal of Political Science, 51*(4), 921–939. http://onlinelibrary.wiley.com/doi/10.1111/j.1540-5907.2007.00289.x/full.

Xiao, V. L. (2022). *Intersectionality at Work: Penalties and Rewards for Breaking or Adhering to Gender Norms across Race.* PhD Dissertation: Stanford University. https://www.proquest.com/dissertations-theses/intersectionality-at-work-penalties-rewards/docview/2786883822/se-2?accountid=13042.

Zellner, H. (1972). Discrimination against Women, Occupational Segregation, and the Relative Wage. *The American Economic Review, 62*(1/2), 157–160. www.jstor.org/stable/1821537.

Acknowledgements

We dedicate this book to Frances McCall Rosenbluth, who, though no longer with us, began this project with us in 2017 and continues to be an inspiration. Frances, we hope you have better things to read, but if not, at least that you enjoy this one.

Cambridge Elements

Gender and Politics

Tiffany D. Barnes
University of Texas at Austin

Tiffany D. Barnes is Professor of Government at University of Texas at Austin. She is the author of *Women, Politics, and Power: A Global Perspective* (Rowman & Littlefield, 2007) and, award-winning, *Gendering Legislative Behavior* (Cambridge University Press, 2016). Her research has been funded by the National Science Foundation (NSF) and recognized with numerous awards. Barnes is the former president of the Midwest Women's Caucus and founder and director of the Empirical Study of Gender (EGEN) network.

Diana Z. O'Brien
Washington University in St. Louis

Diana Z. O'Brien is the Bela Kornitzer Distinguished Professor of Political Science at Washington University in St. Louis. She specializes in the causes and consequences of women's political representation. Her award-winning research has been supported by the NSF and published in leading political science journals. O'Brien has also served as a Fulbright Visiting Professor, an associate editor at *Politics & Gender*, the president of the Midwest Women's Caucus, and a founding member of the EGEN network.

About the Series

From campaigns and elections to policymaking and political conflict, gender pervades every facet of politics. Elements in Gender and Politics features carefully theorized, empirically rigorous scholarship on gender and politics. The Elements both offer new perspectives on foundational questions in the field and identify and address emerging research areas.

Cambridge Elements

Gender and Politics

Elements in the Series

In Love and at War: Marriage in Non-State Armed Groups
Hilary Matfess

Counter-Stereotypes and Attitudes Toward Gender and LGBTQ Equality
Jae-Hee Jung and Margit Tavits

The Politics of Bathroom Access and Exclusion in the United States
Sara Chatfield

Women, Gender, and Rebel Governance during Civil Wars
Meredith Maloof Loken

Abortion Attitudes and Polarization in the American Electorate
Erin C. Cassese, Heather L. Ondercin and Jordan Randall

Gender, Ethnicity, and Intersectionality in Cabinets: Asia and Europe in Comparative Perspective
Amy H. Liu, Roman Hlatky, Keith Padraic Chew, Eoin L. Power, Sam Selsky, Betty Compton and Meiying Xu

Gendered Jobs and Local Leaders: Women, Work, and the Pipeline to Local Political Office
Rachel Bernhard and Mirya R. Holman

A full series listing is available at: www.cambridge.org/EGAP

For EU product safety concerns, contact us at Calle de José Abascal, 56–1°,
28003 Madrid, Spain or eugpsr@cambridge.org.

www.ingramcontent.com/pod-product-compliance
Lightning Source LLC
LaVergne TN
LVHW020333260326
834688LV00037B/1002